HISTORIC FAMILY
HOMES & GARDENS
FROM THE AIR

Over 80 of Britain's
remarkable castles,
houses and gardens
in private ownership with
personal contributions
by their owners

To Robin and Abby with love;
our children and the future

Andy & Brenda Marks
Skyscan

First published in Great Britain in 2003 by

Norman Hudson & Co
High Wardington House
Upper Wardington
Banbury
Oxfordshire OX17 1SP

ISBN 0 - 9531426 - 8 - X

Editors Georgina Bryson and Norman Hudson
Design Karen Cooper (KC Graphics)
Proof reading Jennie Carwithen and Fiona Rolt
Reprographics Spot On Reprographics
Printed by Butler & Tanner Ltd

Contents

HISTORIC HOUSES ASSOCIATION

It has often been said that this country's greatest contribution to European culture is the country house together with art objects, gardens and parks.

In this splendid book 84 such houses are featured. All are privately owned by members of the HHA. All are open to visitors and all are cared for by their owners with minimal or no aid from the State. Many are still at the centre of agricultural estates, the income from which has traditionally maintained the big house. Nowadays many estates have diversified into tourism and other businesses. They continue to be the focus of their surrounding area, providing a venue for a huge range of events such as country fairs and concerts. In the process jobs are provided, families and ancillary businesses and the local economy supported.

Over 12 million visits are made every year to privately owned houses, but many more people visit the gardens and parks surrounding them. Most come for the simple pleasures of fresh air and beautiful scenery but I do urge you to visit as many of the magnificent houses featured here as you can. You will be rewarded by art in all its forms and of the highest quality, all of which reflects so much of this country's long history.

Edward Leicester

The Earl of Leicester
President of the Historic Houses Association

Alnwick Castle

Alnwick, Northumberland

Alnwick Castle occupied a strategic position in the border region between England and Scotland. Following the death of the first Norman Baron of Alnwick, Yvo de Vescy, in 1134, the next two centuries were turbulent times for Alnwick.

It was surrendered to Scotland in 1138, returned to its owner soon after, besieged unsuccessfully by William, the Lion King of Scotland, in 1172 and 1174. In 1213 King John ordered Alnwick to be destroyed after the Barons' Revolt, but thankfully cancelled the order before it was carried out.

The Percies bought Alnwick from the unscrupulous Bishop of Durham in 1309, and for the next 400 years seemed to spend every waking hour fighting the Scots, or the Crown. Few Percy Earls of Northumberland died peacefully in their sleep.

At the end of the 18th century, the Castle and surrounding landscape were transformed by Robert Adam and Lancelot 'Capability' Brown, commissioned by the 1st Duke and Duchess of Northumberland. In the mid 19th century, the 4th Duke engaged Salvin, an Italian architect, to alter completely and modernise the Castle in classical Italian style, creating the wonderful contrast between an austere exterior and a sumptuous interior, full of treasures collected by generations of Percies. Paintings by Canaletto, Van Dyck, Titian, Tintoretto, Turner, Lely and del Sarto, in addition to beautiful collections of furniture, ceramics and books, add to the Castle's appeal.

Outside, overlooking some of the medieval walls, the landscape beyond has changed little for over a hundred years. By contrast, the start of the 21st century has seen the derelict 19th century walled gardens behind the Castle transformed. An enthusiasm of my wife, this has been excitingly redesigned, featuring a huge cascade with spouting water, appealing to both young and old.

Today, the family still live in the Castle. Children run riot and knock into priceless furniture and we all keep fit running up and down hundreds of stairs. It is not the easiest place to live in, but we love it; even though there are times when you cannot avoid the sadder parts of its history. It is hard, for instance, when our dogs are let out onto the grass of the inner bailey for their last pee of the evening, not to think of the 3,000 Scottish prisoners of war who died there.

I hope that visitors to Alnwick Castle feel something of its unique atmosphere, and thoroughly enjoy their visit.

Arbury Hall

Nuneaton, Warwickshire

Arbury, a beautiful house of Elizabethan origin, was built on the site of a 12th century Augustinian priory. It has been the home of the Newdegate family for over 400 years. The house was almost completely 'gothicised' in the 1700s by Sir Roger Newdigate, 5th Baronet, who represented Oxford University in Parliament and founded the Newdigate Prize for Poetry. The principal rooms, with their soaring fan-vaulted ceilings, plunging pendants and filigree tracery, are acknowledged to be the finest complete example of Gothic Revival in existence.

Arbury is home to a fine collection of both oriental and Chelsea porcelain, portraits by Lely, Reynolds, Devis and Romney, and furniture by Chippendale and Hepplewhite, accumulated by successive generations of the Newdegate family. George Eliot, the novelist, was born on the estate at Arbury and Sir Roger was immortalised in her book *Scenes of Clerical Life*. The Stable portico was designed by Sir Christopher Wren and completed c1674.

Standing in its own parkland, Arbury is surrounded by landscaped gardens designed in the picturesque manner of the latter half of the 18th century. With rolling lawns, serpentine paths, carefully sited groups of trees and lakes, the gardens are, like the house, due largely to the influence of Sir Roger Newdigate. In the park, which stretches for a considerable distance beyond the house, a few of the original Forest of Arden oaks can still be found amongst the woods and plantations of the 19th century.

I live at Arbury with my wife and three children. Words cannot describe its wonderful atmosphere, secure and peaceful setting, and scenic backdrop. We enjoy the magnificent house and gardens as a family home and are always pleased to share its extraordinary beauty with all our visitors.

Daventry

Athelhampton House & Gardens

Dorchester, Dorset Patrick Cooke

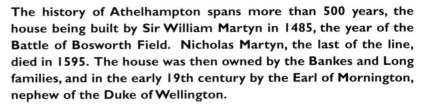

The history of Athelhampton spans more than 500 years, the house being built by Sir William Martyn in 1485, the year of the Battle of Bosworth Field. Nicholas Martyn, the last of the line, died in 1595. The house was then owned by the Bankes and Long families, and in the early 19th century by the Earl of Mornington, nephew of the Duke of Wellington.

In 1891 Alfred Cart de Lafontaine began to restore the house and he built the formal gardens with four courts walled with Ham stone, as well as the two Garden Pavilions. The yew trees in the Great Court were planted at this time and have since grown into topiary pyramids 25' high.

The Church of St John, Athelhampton, built in 1862, was designed by the architect J Hicks of Dorchester, for whom the author Thomas Hardy worked whilst his sister taught at the school opposite. Hardy's poems *The Dame of Athelhall* and *The Children of Sir Nameless* are set at 'Athelhall'. His macabre short story, *The Waiting Supper*, is set in the Great Hall and in the gardens, through which flows the River Piddle.

Both Noël Coward and Douglas Fairbanks were entertained at Athelhampton by Lady Harmsworth in the 1930s. In 1971 the gardens were used for the filming of *Sleuth*, starring Sir Michael Caine and Sir Laurence Olivier. More recently the house and its collections have been featured in many antiques programmes including the BBC *Antiques Roadshow* and in Dr David Starkey's *Elizabeth I* for Channel 4.

My grandfather, Robert V Cooke, a surgeon, moved to Athelhampton in 1957 and the house and garden as they are seen today reflect his influence. He had long resolved to restore an historic house for his collection of fine art and furniture. His work was continued by my father, Sir Robert Cooke, a Member of Parliament whose enthusiasm for the heritage also caused him to be much involved with a major restoration of the Palace of Westminster. Today Athelhampton remains a well-loved and lived-in family home which we enjoy showing to the public.

Patrick Cooke

Beaulieu

Brockenhurst, Hampshire

In June 1204, 30 Cistercian monks from France began the building of Beaulieu Abbey on land gifted by King John in the Royal hunting grounds of the New Forest. The dedication ceremony in 1246 for the completed Abbey church was attended by Henry III, his wife Eleanor and their son the future Edward I.

Beaulieu passed into the ownership of my ancestors in 1538, the year of the Dissolution of the Monasteries, when Sir Thomas Wriothesley, later Earl of Southampton, was granted 'the whole Close of Beaulieu' by Letters Patent, paying £1,340 6s 8d for the 8,000 acre estate.

After 129 years of Wriothesley ownership the estate passed through marriage to the Montagus and John, 2nd Duke of Montagu, inherited in 1709. In the late 18th century, following the 2nd Duke's death, Beaulieu passed through the female line to the Buccleuch family. My great grandfather, the 5th Duke of Buccleuch, gave the Estate to his second son, my grandfather Lord Henry Scott, as a wedding present. He set about extensive alterations to Palace House which remains substantially as he planned it to this day.

In 1951 I succeeded to the Beaulieu Estate on my 25th birthday; until that time a Board of Trustees had managed the estate since my father's death in 1929. My father John was a motoring pioneer and visionary and it was as a tribute to him that I placed five veteran cars in the Entrance Hall of Palace House in 1952 when, in order to help meet the costs of maintaining the many buildings on the estate, I opened the house to visitors. From these modest beginnings grew the world-renowned National Motor Museum.

Sharing my home and welcoming visitors to Beaulieu has been a source of great pleasure to me. I delight in the fact that Palace House and many other buildings on the Estate, are in a better state of repair now than for many decades and their survival for future generations of visitors from all over the world to enjoy is assured.

Montagu of Beaulieu

Belmont

Faversham, Kent

Belmont is an entirely 18th century creation. The first house was built on the site by Edward Wilks in 1769 and survives in part today, as the office wing. The house was then sold in 1780 to Colonel John Montresor who, in 1789, engaged Samuel Wyatt to design and build Belmont as it stands today.

Montresor's career came to an unfortunate end when he was accused, mistakenly, of embezzling Army funds. The Belmont estate was sequestrated by the Government and sold at auction in 1801. It was bought by General George Harris (later 1st Lord Harris), with prize money awarded to him as C-in-C of the British forces that defeated the Tipoo Sultan at the Battle of Seringapatam (4 May 1799) ending French influence in Southern India. The house remained the home of the Harris family until the death of the 5th Lord in 1984 when it passed to the Harris (Belmont) Charity.

The Harris family's record of service to the nation is impressive. The 2nd Lord was a successful Army officer and the 3rd Lord a highly regarded administrator serving as Governor of Trinidad and in Madras during the Indian Mutiny. The 4th Lord Harris combined a career in Government with that of a leading cricketer and administrator during the sport's formative years (1870 – 1930). The 5th Lord devoted his life to the preservation of Belmont and the creation of one of the finest private clock collections in England.

Belmont is important for a number of reasons. Architecturally, it is an unspoilt example of Wyatt's work; historically, it is important for its records and mementoes of the family's careers and lastly, it is distinguished for the magnificent collection of clocks.

The house and garden continue to evolve in the 21st century with the restoration of the large walled Kitchen Garden to the north west of the house in 2001. Designed by Arabella Lennox-Boyd, it features a charming mix of lawns, fruit, vegetables and flowers and an impressive Victorian greenhouse.

Today the house is administered by a Board of Trustees of which, as a direct descendant of the 1st Lord through his second son, I am pleased to be Chairman.

Rear Admiral Michael Harris
Chairman · Harris (Belmont) Charity Trustees

Blair Castle

Pitlochry, Perthshire

When the Atholl family first made their home in Strath Garry more than seven centuries ago, it was a wild and dangerous place. It was also a strategic one. Whoever held Blair Atholl was the gatekeeper to the Grampians and the route north to Inverness.

Over 19 generations the Stewarts and the Murrays of Atholl have made their mark on Blair Castle. The 3rd Earl added a great hall to the Castle where his son, the 4th Earl, welcomed Mary Queen of Scots in 1564. The 5th Earl's grandson became the first Murray Earl of Atholl and the title has remained in the Murray family ever since.

The first Murray Earl's grandson was rewarded with a dukedom in 1703 for supporting the monarch Queen Anne. His son, the 2nd Duke, remodelled the Castle and landscaped the grounds, the work having been interrupted when the Castle was besieged by his younger brother Lord George Murray, commanding the Jacobite campaign.

The 6th Duke entertained Queen Victoria at the Castle in 1844. In appreciation of the guard of Atholl men who attended her, she granted the Duke the right to bear arms. Today the Atholl Highlanders are the only remaining private army in Europe.

Blair Castle has been a magnet to visitors down the generations. To ensure the welcome continues for generations to come, my half-brother, the 10th Duke of Atholl, placed the Castle and surrounding estate into the Blair Charitable Trust in 1995. On his death the following year, the title passed to his cousin who lives in South Africa. Every May he visits the Castle to lead the Atholl Highlanders on their annual parade.

Today the Castle is a busy place, welcoming visitors all year and hosting a variety of events ranging from the three day international horse trials to Easter egg hunts, nature trails and Highland games.

Sarah Troughton

Blairquhan

Maybole, Ayrshire

Since about 1340, there has been a castle at Blairquhan. It has been owned by four families – the McWhirters, the Kennedys, the Whitefoords and, since 1798, the Hunter Blairs. When my great, great grandfather, Sir David Hunter Blair, who was related through his mother to the Kennedys, acquired the Blairquhan estate, the castle was ruinous and barely habitable.

Sir David commissioned the architect William Burn to design a new house which was built slightly to the north of the old castle, between 1821 and 1824. Furniture was supplied by Morison of Ayr and is still in place.

From 1798 onwards, the grounds of Blairquhan were also completely redesigned by Sir David. He planted 1.3 million trees, redirected the River Girvan and diverted the existing public roads to move them further from the castle for a distance of about five miles. New lodges, drives and pathways were constructed, including the famous three mile Long Approach from William Burn's bridge at the Ayr Lodge to the castle.

Blairquhan remains in the possession of the family. My father, the late Sir James Hunter Blair, 7th Baronet, made many additions to the picture collection including a number of works by the Scottish Colourists. The heir to the estate is my cousin, Patrick Hunter Blair, who is presently employed as Chief Planning Officer for the Forestry Department of the Government of Northern Ireland.

James Hunter Blair

Blenheim Palace

Woodstock, Oxfordshire

Almost since Blenheim Palace was built for the 1st Duke of Marlborough in 1705, to celebrate his victory over the French at the Battle of Blenheim in 1704, it has been attracting visitors. The first guidebook for the house was printed in 1787 and in 1802 Admiral Lord Nelson arrived to tour the house with Lady Hamilton. Sir Winston Churchill's mother, Jennie Jerome, describes in her autobiography joining a tour of the house in disguise to hear other visitors' thoughts about the house and about her parents-in-law, the Marlboroughs.

After the Second World War, the house and gardens were opened to the public on a much wider and more regular basis. Like so many of England's historic houses, Blenheim suffered during the war and additional income was badly needed to restore it to its former condition. In April 1950 the doors were opened to the paying public at half a crown (12½p) each with family and friends doing the guiding in the early days.

Blenheim still welcomes visitors to the house for eight months of the year, and its incomparable Park, landscaped by "Capability" Brown, is open most of the year. The setting of the Palace against the matchless beauty of the gardens and park is unforgettable – a breathtaking combination of house and landscape. Blenheim is a national and international treasure, and this was recognised in 1987 when Palace and Park together were declared a World Heritage Site.

The architecture is an unrivalled example of English Baroque, designed by Sir John Vanbrugh, built by craftsmen such as Strong, Townsend and Peisley, and enriched by Grinling Gibbons. Its State Rooms contain important collections of paintings and tapestries, porcelain, sculpture and furniture, as well as family mementoes and photographs. Sir Winston Churchill was born at Blenheim over a hundred years ago, and his memory is celebrated here today in the simple room where he was born, and by an exhibition of his life and work.

Blenheim Palace is not only an important part of Britain's heritage but is still lived in, and greatly cared for, by my family. As the custodian, I endeavour to ensure that this magnificent house and its treasures will be preserved for future generations to visit and enjoy.

Marlborough.

Borde Hill Garden

Haywards Heath, West Sussex

Andrewjohn Stephenson Clarke

Borde Hill has been my family's home since 1893 and each generation has improved and extended the planting, facilities and areas available for public enjoyment. From the early 1900s the garden was planted by my great grandfather, Colonel Stephenson Clarke CBE, with specimens gathered by the great plant expeditions that visited the Himalayas, the Andes, China, Tasmania, Africa and other far-flung parts of the world. Most of the trees and shrubs are fine, often unique, examples with over 100 Champion trees and many years of awards from the Royal Horticultural Society.

Borde Hill has much to offer either the plant enthusiast or those just wanting to learn more about the wide diversity of the horticultural world. They can relax as they walk through the scents and enjoy the colours from the warmth of the Rose Garden to the lush tropical plantings in the Round Dell and the design and space of the Italian Garden. Whether they come to find a rare plant or walk through the rolling Wealden landscape past woods full of bluebells, they will discover something for every taste.

My father, Robert, added many new rhododendrons and garden features and my wife, Eleni, and I have continued to make additions that are very popular with plant lovers and families alike. I recommend the Africa House and the Peach House, both of which are Victorian greenhouses which have been restored with the aid of the Heritage Lottery Fund in a project prompted by the devastation following the Great Storm of 1987.

The garden continues to evolve, offering exciting opportunities for education, entertainment and horticultural variety. Each summer there is open air theatre and concerts staged on the main lawn and in the parkland outside events ranging from garden fairs to equestrian shows and the animal fair are held.

Andrewjohn Stephenson Clarke

Bowood House

Calne, Wiltshire

The original house was built in 1726 by the Bridgeman family and was sold, unfinished, in 1754 to the 1st Earl of Shelburne. The architect Henry Keene was engaged to design a supporting range of buildings behind the main house. In 1762, the 1st Earl's son, William Shelburne, later the Marquis of Lansdowne, employed the leading Scottish architect, Robert Adam, to screen the service courtyards by creating the magnificent Diocletian wing. From that time the original house became known as the Big House and the two courtyards, the Little House.

Not much changed at Bowood during the 19th century apart from construction of the immensely grand Italianate terraces in front of the Diocletian wing. By 1894 the Big House was being used only for entertaining and the family lived in the Little House. This was the situation at the time my father, the 8th Marquis, inherited the estate in 1944 from his cousin, who was killed fighting in Italy. By 1955, the Big House had fallen into such a state of disrepair that the difficult decision was taken to demolish it. Few would now ever know there had been a much larger and dominating building in the south east corner of the front terraces where just a grassy outline remains.

The structure of the park, like the house, has evolved over the past 250 years. 'Capability' Brown drew up a grand design in 1763, some of which was implemented, but by no means all. He created the lake and planted most of the veteran trees still in view of the house today. The pinetum and arboretum were well established by the mid 19th century – during the 3rd Marquis' tenure – an exciting time for introducing some of the rare trees being brought back to England by Victorian dendrologists. The 5th Marquis was a passionate plantsman and established the rhododendron garden. Each successive generation has continued to plant and enhance the beauty of the estate. Between 1972 and 2002 over 300,000 trees have been planted in or surrounding the park.

During the last 20 years we have created an exciting adventure playground to the north west of the house. This has proved enormously popular with children. More recently, a golf course has been made in the far west of the park, without detracting from the historic landscape. Visitors will find Bowood an enchanting oasis where man's vision and sensitivity have harnessed nature's fragile and dynamic forces to create perfect harmony.

Lansdowne

The Marquis of Lansdowne

Breamore House

Fordingbridge, Hampshire

Situated at the edge of the New Forest, Breamore House was completed in 1583 as an Elizabethan manor house for William Dodington. Built of rose red brick and faced with stone, it has changed little over the years. It has the typical two outer gables and the smaller central gable forming the letter 'E'.

William Dodington, in anxiety over an impending law suit, "*went up to St. Sepulchre's Steeple, threw himself over the battlements and brake his neck*". William was Queen Elizabeth's Treasurer or, in modern parlance, Chancellor of the Exchequer. His suicide, in broad daylight on 11th April 1600, caused a sensation in Elizabethan London. His son William was knighted by James I in 1603 but fate was again unkind – in 1629 Lady Dodington was murdered by their son Henry in Breamore House. He was hanged a year later and the property passed to his sister, Anne, who married Lord Brooke. Their son was created Earl of Warwick, and sold the property to Sir Edward Hulse, son of Dr Edward Hulse, in 1748.

The Hulse family arrived from Holland with William and Mary in 1688, Dr Edward Hulse being physician to William of Orange. Their ownership of Breamore brought happier times to the house following the previous 50 years of rather grisly history and associations. The house in which we live today remains essentially a family home containing the collections of ten generations of my family. There are excellent pictures which include many Dutch paintings, a Canaletto and a fascinating collection of 14 Mexican caste paintings by Juan Rodrigues Jarez. An early cricketing picture, the '*Boy with a bat*', was exhibited in the National Gallery in Washington as part of the blockbuster *Treasure Houses of Britain* exhibition in 1979. We are fortunate also to have in the house some good furniture, and also china from around the world.

In the former kitchen garden, we have created a Countryside Museum, recalling a time when a rural village was self-sufficient.

Edward Hulse

Sir Edward Hulse Bt

Broughton Castle

Banbury, Oxfordshire

In about 1300 Sir John de Broughton built his manor house and surrounded it with a substantial moat. In 1377 the house was bought by William of Wykeham, Bishop of Winchester, Chancellor of England and founder of New College, Oxford. It then passed to his great-nephew Sir Thomas Wykeham and thence to Sir Thomas' grand-daughter, Margaret, who married Sir William Fiennes, later 2nd Lord Saye and Sele, in 1448. Broughton has therefore been in the continuous ownership of the same family since 1377.

Sir Thomas Wykeham obtained a licence to 'crenellate and embattle' in 1406, giving the medieval house a military appearance. Even so, the present title of castle is misleading, if by that is meant a place of great strength or one devoted to military purposes.

In 1554 Richard Fiennes completed a reconstruction in the 'Court' style of Edward VI. After his death in 1573 his son, Richard, continued the embellishment of the interior, and the medieval manor house was thus transformed into a Tudor mansion. This building activity of the 16th century gave way to political activity in the 17th century when William, 8th Lord Saye and Sele, played a leading role in national affairs, being strongly opposed to Charles I's efforts to rule without Parliament.

The 18th century was, by contrast, uneventful but in the 19th century William Thomas, son of the 14th Baron, indulged in a life of frivolity and extravagance as one of the set surrounding the Prince Regent and the Count d'Orsay. The house was allowed to fall into a state of neglect and, in 1837, the bulk of the contents of the castle were disposed of in an eight-day sale, the last item being the swans on the moat.

It is a strange irony that the squandering of the family fortune in the Regency period almost certainly saved Broughton from the architectural excesses of the Victorian age. William Thomas' successors, Frederick, 16th Lord Saye and Sele and Archdeacon of Hereford, carried out vital repair work in the 1860s under the direction of the architect George Gilbert Scott. The past 50 years at Broughton have been a period of major restoration, starting first with renewal of the stone-tiled roof and continuous stonework restoration between 1983-1994 at a cost of £1 million, towards which English Heritage gave generous aid.

Saye & Sele.

Lord Saye and Sele

Burton Agnes Hall

Driffield, Yorkshire

The Burton Agnes Hall Preservation Trust Ltd

Burton Agnes Hall is a magnificent example of Elizabethan architecture, built in 1598 by Sir Henry Griffith. The architect was Robert Smithson. It is still lived in by descendants of the same family, having passed through the female line on a number of occasions. The house is filled with treasures collected and commissioned by the family over the centuries. The original Elizabethan carving and plasterwork still decorate many rooms, while there are some lovely examples of Georgian furniture and porcelain, and a marvellous collection of modern French and English paintings of the Impressionist Schools. We are continuing to add to the collections and the latest commissions include a tapestry by Kaffe Fassett, embroidery by Janet Haigh and four pieces of furniture by John Makepeace.

Beside the present hall is the old Norman manor house, now encased in brick, but you can still see the lower chamber with its massive piers and groined and vaulted roof and the Great Hall above.

During the 20th century, the Hall and gardens underwent two restorations. Having inherited the house from his mother in 1947, Marcus Wickham-Boynton did a great deal of work on the house including a complete restoration of the Long Gallery which runs the length of the house on the top floor. This had fallen into disrepair at the beginning of the 19th century when the plaster ceiling had fallen in. In 1977 Marcus Wickham-Boynton put the house and grounds into a Charitable Trust. On his death in 1989, the estate and care of the house passed to a cousin, Simon Cunliffe-Lister. At the time he was only 12 so I, his mother, am chatelaine of the house pro-tem. On coming to Burton Agnes in 1990, I started on a restoration of the Walled Garden. This now contains much to interest plant lovers as well as entertain young and old alike. There is a Maze, Jungle Garden, Potager and giant board games in coloured gardens.

Susan Cunliffe-Lister

Castle Howard

York, North Yorkshire

My family originate from Lord William Howard (1563-1640), youngest son of Thomas, 4th Duke of Norfolk, whose skill at marrying heiresses eventually led to his execution! 'Belted Will' as Lord William Howard was known, took possession of Henderskelfe in Yorkshire, the site of Castle Howard today and it was his great, great, great grandson, Charles, 3rd Earl of Carlisle, who created Castle Howard.

The celebrated architects Sir John Vanbrugh and Nicholas Hawksmoor were commissioned to design and build the house, and between 1699 and 1714 two-thirds of the house was completed. It remained unfinished for the rest of the 3rd Earl's life as he concentrated on building other follies in the grounds including obelisks, pyramids, the Temple of the Four Winds and, ultimately, the Mausoleum. He died in 1738 and the 4th Earl attempted to finish the house, employing his brother-in-law, Sir Thomas Robinson. The wing was finally completed and decorated by the 5th Earl, by 1811.

The house continued to pass from one Earl of Carlisle to another until 1921 when the family estates were divided according to liberal principles and the house and estate passed to The Hon Geoffrey Howard, my grandfather. He died in 1935 and the house and estate were then administered by a family trust, none of the children being of age.

George Howard, my father who, returning wounded from the war, decided against all expectation to move into the house and vigorously set about revitalising and restoring its spirit and fabric. In 1949 he married my mother, Lady Cecilia Fitzroy, daughter of the 8th Duke of Grafton. Together they opened the house and grounds in 1952 and his life was then divided between public service and devotion to the continuance of Castle Howard. He was created a life peer in 1983, taking the title Lord Howard of Henderskelfe, only to die in 1984.

Today the house and estate are owned and administered by a private company of which my brother, Nicholas and I are the directors. Occupation of the house by the family (in this generation by my wife Rebecca and I, and our twins, Octavia and Merlin) is made possible by constantly adapting to change and pursuing a forward-thinking and structured business policy. We hope that many generations will continue to enjoy the house both inside and out, for many centuries to come.

The Hon Simon Howard
Chairman – Castle Howard Estate Limited

Cawdor Castle

Nairn, Inverness-shire

This splendid and romantic castle, dating from the 14th century, was originally the fortress home of the Thanes of Cawdor. The oldest part, approached by a drawbridge, is the central tower built round the legendary holly tree. Later additions to the Castle, carried out over succeeding centuries, were all built in the Scottish vernacular manner of defensive architecture: steep slated roofs with crow-stepped gables and strong walls of local stone.

The Castle has evolved over a period of 600 years, during which time the small, grim tower house was transformed into a generous, charming family mansion. The skyline of turrets and battlements delights children with its fairy-tale aspect and yet a rather severe, even a fictional, exterior belies an enchanting interior where private taste has evidently meant more than public fashion.

Cawdor is fortunate to have three gardens. The Flower Garden has a family feel to it, where plants are chosen out of affection rather than affectation. This is a lovely spot between spring and late summer. The Wild Garden beside its stream leads on to beautiful trails through a spectacular mature mixed woodland. The Walled Garden, comprising a holly maze, paradise garden, knot garden and orchard, has been restored over the last 20 years to recreate a 16th century atmosphere, the date of the garden walls.

Visitors comment that there is a friendly atmosphere about the place in which good furniture, fine portraits, distinctive pictures, interesting objects and outstanding tapestries are arranged in a relaxed, informal way: this is a home, not a museum. A medieval turnpike stair, a dungeon and an ancient freshwater well are features that all echo dark and dismal days; memories of Shakespeare's *Macbeth* return theatrically. Features like these give Cawdor an elusive, evocative quality and a unique character that no visitor, young or old, can forget.

Angelika Cawdor

The Dowager Countess Cawdor

Chavenage

Tetbury, Gloucestershire

David Lowsley-Williams

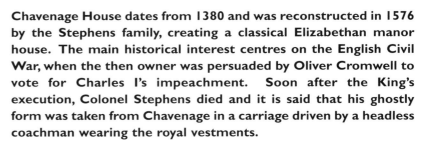

Chavenage House dates from 1380 and was reconstructed in 1576 by the Stephens family, creating a classical Elizabethan manor house. The main historical interest centres on the English Civil War, when the then owner was persuaded by Oliver Cromwell to vote for Charles I's impeachment. Soon after the King's execution, Colonel Stephens died and it is said that his ghostly form was taken from Chavenage in a carriage driven by a headless coachman wearing the royal vestments.

Chavenage is situated in the heart of the Cotswolds, set in 1500 acres of privately-owned land. My grandfather bought the house and estate in 1891 adding, at the turn of the century, the Edwardian wing which incorporates a Ball Room with a sprung floor, built under the Arts and Crafts influence. Close to the house is the 18th century family chapel.

The house has been used for several film and TV locations and visitors may recognise it from such programmes as *Poirot*, *Cider with Rosie*, *Berkeley Square*, *House of Elliot*, *Casualty* and *Grace and Favour*.

"*Sorry about the children's bicycles barring the way into the front door of the house*" is a frequent greeting visitors receive at Chavenage. When acting as guide, which, as a frustrated thespian I rather enjoy, I am often embarrassed by evidence that the house is still very much the family home, a fact which is much of the charm of Chavenage. Having negotiated the free-range bantams which guard the entrance from the car park, visitors find themselves being greeted by four spaniels before meeting any of the family. The estate is a family-run affair; my son George runs the farming enterprises, my wife Rona oversees the dairy operation, Caroline, my elder daughter is the administrator for the House business and Joanna, her younger sister, is in charge of the catering. Recently, Chavenage has proved to be a popular venue for wedding receptions – often there are 30 in a year – the only downside being having to deal with 30 brides' mothers!

David Lowsley-Williams

David Lowsley-Williams

Chiddingstone Castle

Edenbridge, Kent

In 1550 the Streatfeilds, wealthy ironmasters of unknown provenance, settled in Chiddingstone, occupying an ancient house on what is now the site of Chiddingstone Castle.

Little is known of their dwellings until 1803, when Squire Henry Streatfeild commissioned William Atkinson to build a castle-style residence for him. Henry was devoured by the passion for medieval chivalry then sweeping England. Atkinson's design for a new south carriage entrance was exhibited at the Royal Academy Exhibition in 1805 and can be seen there today, still in excellent condition.

Atkinson's concept for the complete castle was unique. It was also his first important commission and is interesting because he would never again attempt anything on such a *small* scale or such sheer romantic fantasy. According to his custom, he used local materials and the enormous blocks used to construct the castle were quarried from a special site in the grounds – now flooded as a lake. Work on the castle proceeded at a hectic pace until about 1808, and then stopped. The design was never completed.

The Streatfeilds continued to live in the castle until the death of the last squire, Sir Henry, in 1938. The heir apparent detested the place, emigrating eventually to Vienna, and the castle was sold. By the time Denys Bower bought it in 1955 it was in a semi-derelict state, having suffered much neglect during and after the Second World War. Bower had no spare cash for repairs – he spent his all on collecting. He was the most remarkable collector since Beckford – indeed more so, for Beckford had money and he had none. His document collection of Stuart Papers is second only to that of Windsor Castle and his Japanese lacquer is the finest in the West.

When he died, Denys Bower left everything to the Nation "*so that future generations may enjoy them as I do now*". He believed that works of art should be enjoyed not in a museum, but at home. For nearly 30 years, I and my co-trustees have struggled to achieve Bower's wishes. We are in sight of our goal and the castle has never been in better condition, or more beautiful or homely. This is indeed a miracle worth seeing.

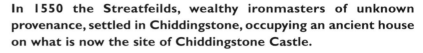

Ruth Eldridge

Ruth Eldridge MBE
Managing Trustee

Cholmondeley Castle Gardens

Malpas, Cheshire

The gardens at Cholmondeley must have been first laid out at the time the Castle was built by the 1st Marquess of Cholmondeley on top of what was then known as Fir Hill.

The original site of the ancient home of the Cholmondeley family is in the park near to the walled gardens. During the reign of Queen Anne, the 1st Earl decided to rebuild on the site in a grander style and employed the fashionable architect, Sir John Vanbrugh. The house became very neglected during the life of the 3rd Earl and the 1st Marquess decided that a new home should be built, this time on higher ground away from the damp which affected the low-lying land. The baroque and Palladianism being out of fashion, Lord Cholmondeley had the house built to his own design in 'romantic gothick' style between 1801-1804. Robert Smirke, architect of the British Museum, was employed by him in 1817 to embellish the house further and the present outline of the Castle took shape and has hardly altered since.

The grounds at that time were filled with laurel, bamboos and large plantings of the commoner types of rhododendrons which, on our arrival, had become the size of haystacks. The two fine specimens of cedar of Lebanon may well have been planted on the slope in front of the Castle at the start of the 19th century, or even earlier. By the time my husband and I came to Cholmondeley in 1950, we found the grounds well cared for but, apart from the beautiful trees, very little planting of interest. However, owing to shortage of labour and an abundance of rabbits, there was little we could do beyond making a new vegetable garden, a rose garden and a double herbaceous border (fenced in against the rabbits!).

The late Brian McKenna was employed to rebuild and replant the waterfall rock garden in the Temple Garden. Then, in 1960, with the help of James Russell, the well-known landscape gardener, we developed the artistic potential of the gardens and planted many rhododendrons, trees and shrubs in the grounds, groups of trees in the park, redesigned the herbaceous borders and restored the lake in the Temple Garden and the stream leading to it.

Lavinia Cholmondeley

48

Cothay Manor

Wellington, Somerset

Alastair Robb / Mary-Anne Robb

Cothay lies near nowhere on the Somerset/Devon borders. It was built at the end of the Wars of the Roses in 1485 and said by the historian, Christopher Hussey, to be *"the finest example of an untouched, small medieval manor remaining in the kingdom"*. Today Cothay looks much as it must have done when Sir Richard Bluett moved from nearby Kittesford and enlarged the 12th century hall house built by the de Cothays. The Bluetts remained at Cothay until 1605 when they sold to the Every family. William Every died in 1679 and thereafter, for the best part of 200 years, it was let to various tenants. Cothay was conveyed away from the Every family in 1796.

The manor, a classic late medieval structure, with its 14th century porch and oratory above; the angel corbelled Great Hall, many wall paintings, the original 15" key in the Great Hall Door, the high screen on the screens gallery, marvellous 17th century oak wainscotting painted to look like walnut, and the richly decorated Great Chamber, all evoke the atmosphere and romance of the age.

The gardens, laid out in the 1920s by Colonel Reginald Cooper DSO, are a plantsman's paradise. Sitting on the banks of the River Tone, the gardens have been restored over the last ten years within the original framework of a 200 yard Yew Walk, off which there are many garden rooms. On the wall of the house by the terrace is a red and white rose. Legend has it that the original was planted to commemorate the end of the Wars of the Roses. This plantsman's 12 acre garden comprises seven garden rooms – herbaceous borders, White Garden, Terrace Garden, Emily's Garden, Cherry Garden, Bishop's Garden and the Walk of the Unicorn. Outside the rooms are a Bog Garden, Cottage Garden and 5 acres of specimen trees.

The setting and age of Cothay add to its romance for here, in medieval times, the rent for the land was a pair of silver spurs and a single red rose, payable on the Feast of St John the Baptist.

Alastair Robb

M. A. Robb.

Alastair Robb / Mary-Anne Robb

Cottesbrooke Hall & Gardens

Cottesbrooke, Northamptonshire

In 1635 the Cottesbrooke Estate was acquired by James Langham, who had progressed from very humble beginnings in Guilsborough (a local village) to become Lord Mayor of London. It was his grandson, Sir John Langham, 4th Bt, who built the house during the reign of Queen Anne. However the identity of the original architect remains a matter for speculation, although Smith of Warwick is very likely. The house has remained essentially the same since that time. The Langham family continued to live at Cottesbrooke until early in the 20th century.

During the Second World War many children were evacuated to Cottesbrooke village and The Grange served as a convalescent hospital for wounded servicemen, whilst the Hall housed the collection of stuffed birds from the British Museum! Many of the people who live in the village of Cottesbrooke and those who work on the estate are second and third generation villagers.

The Hall has much fine furniture, porcelain, bronzes and statues but its chief distinction is the Woolavington Collection of sporting pictures containing works by most of the finest equestrian and sporting painters. This collection was formed principally by my grandfather, Sir James Buchanan Bt, afterwards Lord Woolavington.

Architecturally the main staircase and hall may be judged as the finest features inside the house. The stairs are made of Northamptonshire marble and the walls are decorated in rococo *papier maché* which is extremely rare in England, although much was exported, particularly to America.

The 18th century landscaping of the Park, its vistas and lakes, are by an unknown hand, and much has been restored in recent years. The formal and wild gardens surrounding and adjacent to the house have been mainly developed during the last century and a number of distinguished landscape designers have been involved. But the main inspiration came from my mother, the late Lady Macdonald-Buchanan. At the same time a number of distinguished landscape designers were involved, including Robert Weir Shultz, Sir Geoffrey Jellicoe and Dame Sylvia Crowe. My wife and I have endeavoured to continue these developments. We were extremely pleased when, in 2000, the Gardens were voted winner of the HHA/Christie's 'Garden of the Year' Award.

My family and I consider that we are especially fortunate to live at Cottesbrooke, both in the house and for its surroundings. We hope that visitors to Cottesbrooke share our pleasure in both the house and gardens of which we are so fond and proud.

John Macdonald-Buchanan

J Macdonald-Buchanan

Coughton Court

Alcester, Warwickshire

Clare Throckmorton

The Throckmortons came to Coughton in 1409 when John de Throckmorton married into the de Spiney family. Coughton Court, as we know it today, was built c1530 and the Tudor Gatehouse is still its outstanding architectural feature. The Courtyard has Elizabethan half-timbering on the side walls and originally it had a fourth (East) wing which was burnt down by an angry Protestant mob from the local town of Alcester in 1688.

The Throckmorton family have always maintained their Roman Catholic faith and suffered for it by persecutions in the time of Queen Elizabeth I, culminating in the Gunpowder Plot of 1605 – two of the leading plotters, Catesby and Tresham, were grandsons of Sir Robert Throckmorton. The family were leaders in Catholic Emancipation and Sir Robert (the 8th Baronet) was the first Roman Catholic MP to take his seat in the House of Commons in the early 19th century.

The Abdication letter of Edward VIII came into the possession of the family as Mr Geoffrey Throckmorton was Clerk of the Journals of the House of Commons in 1936 and in those days it was the Clerk's 'perks' to keep the Sovereign's correspondence.

Coughton Court is full of history, illustrated by family portraits and memorabilia ranging from the chemise worn by Mary, Queen of Scots at her execution; a priest's cope embroidered by Queen Katherine of Aragon and her ladies; to the Throckmorton coat, the result of a 1,000 guinea wager by Sir John Throckmorton in 1811. A number of famous artists completed portraits of the Throckmortons, from Tudor panel portraits to my portrait of 1996.

There are many family stories. The earliest recorded one is that when Sir George Throckmorton challenged Henry VIII's wish to marry Ann Boleyn, he accused him of 'meddling' with both her mother and sister. The King replied "*Never with the mother*" but the courtiers had to add "*nor with the sister*" to save the Sovereign's face.

The 10th Baronet, like many of his predecessors, had a large young family. One day the under-nursemaid, neglectful of her charges, allowed the baby to crawl off the bed into a slop pail, where she drowned. Sir Richard called for her and said "*Nell, if you do that again, you'll have to go*".

Since inheriting in 1989, I have been refurbishing the house and, with assistance from my garden designer daughter Christina, have created a new 25 acre garden.

Clare Throckmorton

Deene Park

Corby, Northamptonshire

Sir Robert Brudenell was the first of my family to take up residence at Deene in 1514. He was Chief Justice of the Court of Common Pleas which gave him influence as Deene was then owned by the Abbot of Westminster, to whom a fee farm rent was paid until the late 20th century. He had earlier married into a Leicestershire family and much of those lands remain part of the Estates to this day. His grandson, Sir Edmund, built the Great Hall of 1571 with its magnificent sweet chestnut hammerbeam roof, and successive generations of my family have both added and demolished parts of the house thereby achieving the Tudor and Regency mansion of today.

Since my father's death in 1962, approximately a quarter of the house has been removed, principally a Georgian laundry and the Ballroom which was built by the 7th Earl of Cardigan in celebration of his heroism in the Crimea at Balaklava in 1854. Although the Ballroom no longer forms an addition at the western side of the house, we have many relics and artefacts relating to Lord Cardigan's military career, including uniforms and the head of his charger, Ronald, who carried him in battle and bore him to the grave.

We have also developed the gardens over recent years including a parterre on the south lawn, added in 1990 to a design by the late David Hicks, who was also instrumental in the planning of our Millennium obelisk.

The house is thankfully now in better order than it has been for 150 years but it has taken time and some persistence to achieve this. It has been heartening to hear the reaction of others and we both very much enjoy sharing our home with visitors. I am reassured to think that the family's interest and care will extend through future generations including our young grandson, William, despite the rapidly changing world around us.

Edmund Brudenell

Dorney Court

Windsor, Berkshire

The most southerly parish in Buckinghamshire, Dorney lies on a slight rise of the Thames flood plain – the ancient fields having never been enclosed they can be seen today much as they were in mediaeval times. Dorney Common itself has not changed in 500 years and is still fully used by those with Common rights.

Dorney Court has been the home of our family since 1620 and before that, through marriage, to the Garrards since 1537. This long period of continuous family occupation of over 450 years is rare, especially in a village manor not far from London.

The Great Hall is a superb example of Tudor architecture. Two portraits of the Earl and Countess of Castlemaine by Lely preside over the fireplace, with 13 generations of family portraits around them. The beautiful linenfold panelling was once in Faversham Abbey and the fireplace, brought from elsewhere, is earlier than the Hall itself. This room was also used to hold the Manor Court which legally can still be held here today.

The large carved stone pineapple standing to one side of the Great Hall commemorates the first pineapple ever to be grown in England, here at Dorney Court. The story is that at a dinner in the Mansion House, Charles II cut the top off a pineapple which had been brought from Barbados and gave it to Roger Palmer, Earl of Castlemaine. His gardener, Rose, planted the top and the resulting pineapple was duly presented to the King in 1661.

The rooms are atmospheric and full of history, with early 15th and 16th century oak and 17th century lacquer furniture alongside stained glass and needlework. Adjacent to the house is the 14th century Church of St James the Less, with its Norman font and Tudor tower.

Since opening the house in 1981 an enormous amount has been done towards restoring pictures, furniture and the fabric – the work is never ending but incredibly rewarding. With the help and enthusiasm of my three sons, I very much intend to continue with the restoration work until the time is right for the next generation to succeed!

Jill Palmer

Duart Castle

Isle of Mull, Argyll

Duart Castle has been the home of the Macleans since Lachlan Maclean, the 5th Chief, married Margaret Macdonald, the daughter of the Lord of the Isles, in 1360. Duart and the surrounding lands were granted to the Macleans as a dowry. Lachlan almost certainly built the keep on the outside of the existing courtyard walls and enclosed the well.

During the following 200 years the range of buildings within the original courtyard, on the east and north sides, were completed. Sir Allan Maclean made the most recent alteration to these buildings in 1673 and his crest, rather worn, is still above the door, his initials just discernible.

From the sea room window, you can see at low tide the rock where the 11th Chief abandoned his wife, expecting her to drown. She had failed to produce an heir. She was, however, rescued by passing fishermen and taken to her brother, the Earl of Argyll, at Inverarary Castle. Lachlan arrived to tell him of his sister's tragic death only to find his wife dining with the Earl! However, the Campbells soon took their revenge when, in 1523, Lachlan was murdered on a visit to Edinburgh.

The Macleans were staunch royalists and fought for King Charles II throughout the Cromwellian War and again for the Stuarts in the risings of 1715 and 1745. In 1653 Duart was attacked by English warships, sent to capture the 10 year old chief. Fortunately he had been taken to to the Treshnish Isles for safety.

After this, the Macleans lost Duart and all their lands were forfeited in 1691. The Castle, in rather a ruinous condition, was used as a garrison for a short time. Just beside the Castle, the wives and children of these soldiers are buried in a small graveyard especially consecrated for this purpose.

For over 150 years, the Castle was a ruin until my great grandfather, Sir Fitzroy, purchased it in 1910 and engaged the architect, Sir John Burnett, to undertake its restoration. Sir Fitzroy was nearly 70 when the repairs were finished just before the First World War began. He lived at Duart for most of the time until his death in 1936, in his 101st year.

Duart is still our family home.

Sir Lachlan Maclean Bt

Duncombe Park

Helmsley, North Yorkshire

Duncombe Park is a baroque mansion built for Sir Charles Duncombe to the designs of William Wakefield c1713. It is likely that Sir John Vanbrugh acted as an adviser, as he was working at about the same time for the Earl of Carlisle at neighbouring Castle Howard.

Like most great houses, Duncombe Park has undergone a number of alterations since it was built. The original wings were replaced in 1843 to the designs of Sir Charles Barry and the main block, gutted by fire in 1879, was restored in 1895 by William Young, largely to the original design.

Sir Charles Duncombe, Lord Mayor of London in 1708, pursued a career as a goldsmith and banker. Having amassed a vast fortune, he purchased the Helmsley estate from the executors of George Villiers, 2nd Duke of Buckingham, for what at the time was a record sum of money in a transaction for land. Lord Macaulay, in his 'History of England', noted: "*In a few years a palace more splendid and costly than had ever been inhabited by the magnificent Villiers, rose amidst the beautiful woods and waters which had been his*". Sir Charles died without children and his fortune was divided between a niece and two nephews, one of whom was my ancestor. The family moved out of the house after the First World War and it was subsequently let for use as a girls' school for 64 years. In 1986, my wife and I decided to return and restore the house once again as our family home.

The house is set in the most beautiful park, a royal deer park following the Norman Conquest, and now a national nature reserve containing many ancient oak trees, survivors from the Middle Ages. The river Rye meanders between the steeply wooded slopes of the valley below the house, which is set in an 18th century landscape garden described by Sacheverell Sitwell as "*the supreme masterpiece of the art of the landscape gardener*", and by the late Christopher Hussey as "*perhaps the most spectacularly beautiful among English landscape conceptions of the 18th century*".

Feversham

Dunrobin Castle

Golspie, Sutherland

Dating from the early 1300s, Dunrobin Castle, ancestral home of the Clan Sutherland, is one of the oldest continuously inhabited houses in Britain. My mother, the Countess of Sutherland, retains apartments within the Castle. In 1845 Sir Charles Barry, having just completed the new Houses of Parliament, was employed to re-model the early Castle into a massive baronial residence, inspired by Queen Victoria's new house at Balmoral.

Queen Victoria visited Dunrobin in 1872 and the tapestries on the walls in the Ladies Sitting Room were commissioned in honour of her visit. Harriet, Duchess of Sutherland, wife of the 2nd Duke of Sutherland, was Mistress of the Robes to Queen Victoria at the time of her coronation in 1838.

Much of Barry's interior was destroyed by a disastrous fire in 1915 and the leading Scottish architect, Sir Robert Lorimer, was called in to redesign all the main rooms. The principal rooms include the Drawing Room, where hangs a fine set of Mortlake tapestries and a series of Alenetsev's paintings of Venice, the Green and Gold Room, Lorimer's sycamore Library, containing over 10,000 volumes, and a contemporary portrait of Duchess Eileen by Philip de Lazlo. The Castle is most noted for its collection of 18th and 19th century portraits, as well as a series of earlier portraits of the Earls of Sutherland.

The Victorian Museum, formerly a summer house, contains an outstanding collection of big game trophies, a unique collection of Pictish stones and other items of local history, ornithology, geology and ethnography.

The Castle has exceptional formal gardens, again designed by Barry over 150 years ago. They contain some of the few remaining formal parterres in the French style, though with a definite Scottish flavour. There is an outstanding falconry display in the gardens.

There are lovely walks from the Castle past the Old Mill and up the Big Burn behind Golspie. These were created in the 19th century and have been restored and maintained by a local society.

Alistair Strathnaver

Dunvegan Castle

Isle of Skye

Dunvegan Castle on the Isle of Skye is the oldest castle in Scotland continuously inhabited by the same family since the beginning of recorded time – in these parts some 800 years ago.

'*Un chateau fort*' as the French would say, it was only in 1748 that the first landward entrance was created. Until then the only access entailed climbing a flight of rough stone steps from the sea to a heavily fortified gate at the base of the perimeter wall. Behind the gate lurked a portcullis protecting a steep, narrow, right-angled corridor, from the walls of which the defenders could easily account for any unwanted visitor. Today my family and I are glad to share with the many thousands of visitors to the castle the truth that entering it through the 18th century front door is very much more comfortable.

Throughout the centuries the castle has been a living witness to the history of the Gaelic experience. The years of dislike, verging on hatred, for the culture of the clans shown by such luminaries as James Stuart VI of Scotland and the Scottish Establishment in Edinburgh, culminated in the destruction of the clan system after the 1745 Jacobite Uprising. Therefore the articles of beauty and fascination, which still remain within the castle, hold a special and profound meaning for the Chief and his Clan. The building of the castle, holding within it such famous objects as the Fairy Flag, Ruaraidh Mhor's Horn, the MacCrimmon pipes, the Dunvegan Cup, and a particularly beautiful collection of family portraits, offers a unique insight into the culture and history of the Gael.

After centuries of strife Dunvegan is glad now to be living in a time of peace. It is fitting that the significant changes just preceding the Millennium have occurred outwith the castle walls, notable in the reclamation from the sun, rain, winds and mists of Skye of a splendid garden, creating an atmosphere of peace and beauty much appreciated by family and visitors alike. I look forward to welcoming all those who wish to enjoy the romance of Dunvegan Castle, its gardens and its loch.

John MacLeod of MacLeod

John MacLeod of MacLeod

Eastnor Castle

Ledbury, Herefordshire

Eastnor has been owned by the Somers Cocks family and their descendants, the Hervey-Bathursts, since 1600, but the Castle dates from 1812 when the 1st Earl Somers commissioned the architect, Robert Smirke, to replace a rambling manor house with this altogether much grander mansion. Completed in 1818, Eastnor has been in almost continual family occupation since then, and today the private apartments are still home to my family.

The 1st Earl Somers was related to the Lord Chancellor Somers (d1716), a prominent Whig politician and lawyer, who promoted, inter alia, the Glorious Revolution (1688), the Declaration of Rights and the Act of Union with Scotland (1707). He was also a great collector and the 1st Earl inevitably felt the family's achievements and status should be recognised by a house on a more imposing scale. Lady Henry Somerset, to whom Eastnor passed on the death of the 3rd Earl (1883), was an ardent worker for women's rights and devoted much of her life to charitable works.

The Castle is built in a neo-Norman style, a glorious dream of medieval chivalry, with commanding views up to the Malvern Hills. From a distance, it is intended to give the impression of being another of the Edward I fortresses of the Welsh Marches; it is also a massive statement of aristocratic self-confidence and defiance in the face of the revolutionary movements and political unrest of the time. This spirit is also reflected in the scale of the principal state rooms, especially the Entrance Hall and Great Hall: the use of cast iron beams (due a shortage of timber thanks to the demands of the Royal Navy at the time) enabled these spaces to be created with unusual ease.

Although Smirke designed most of the interiors to be consistent with his original vision, the Drawing Room was refurbished in the neo-Gothic style by Pugin in 1849. Turkish daggers, Scottish broadswords, the remains of an Etruscan helmet (c440 BC) and over 30 suits of armour are among the contents which also include tapestries, paintings and Italian furniture. All parts open to visitors have, in recent years, been the subject of extensive restoration and much of the exterior has been repaired with support from English Heritage.

James Hervey Bathurst.

James Hervey-Bathurst

Eyam Hall

Hope Valley, Derbyshire

This small but charming manor house in the centre of the famous "plague village" of Eyam has been the home of the Wright family since 1671 and it retains the intimate atmosphere of a much loved private home.

The first owners of Eyam Hall, John and Elizabeth, received the house as a wedding present from John's father, Thomas Wright. Although the carved hearts on the finials of the beautiful oak staircase would lead one to think of romance, the reality is likely to be much more prosaic in the form of an arranged marriage between John and the wealthy heiress Elizabeth! Elizabeth still gazes rather severely at her descendants from her portrait in the Hall, whereas her great grandson, Major John Wright, who was ADC to General Burgoyne during the American War of Independence, has a more jovial air.

A pair of unusual bacon settles still have pride of place either side of the fireplace, where they have stood for 330 years. Anyone expecting to find flitches of bacon on opening them would be disappointed however, since they have become a useful repository for the family's hats, gloves, walking boots and light bulbs.

A visit to the Tapestry Room reveals a remarkable interior, literally wallpapered with tapestries, ranging from a fine 15th century Flemish tapestry worked in wool and silk, to a patchwork of 11 pieces of tapestry depicting pastoral scenes.

Some Wright gentlemen were romantic as the highly sentimental poem to Fanny Holme engraved on the Library window by Robert Wright suggests. She remains something of a mystery however, as although Robert married twice, neither time was it to Fanny!

I inherited the house in 1990 and, together with my wife Nicola and our three children, have carried out a sympathetic and thorough restoration. The house is full of family portraits, embroidery, china, glass, silver and costume. The restoration of the walled garden is underway and designs by Nicola and gardener John Pitts for the newly planted knot garden are beginning to take shape.

In addition to opening to the public during the summer months, Eyam Hall is also licensed for Civil weddings. A programme of musical events, a delightful craft centre, a shop and a restaurant keep us busy throughout the year.

Robert Wright

70

Fasque

Laurencekirk, Kincardineshire

The story of Fasque began in 1809 when Sir Alexander Ramsay demolished a modest and graceful 18th century house, which stood about 50 yards to the north of the current house, and replaced it with a much bigger and more palatial building. This ambitious act was one of several factors that led to his financial downfall and he was forced to sell his new house only 20 years after completion. The house was bought in 1829 by my great, great grandfather, John Gladstone, the eldest son of Thomas Gladstone, a corn merchant from Leith.

John Gladstone, an eminent businessman and politician in his own right, came to live at Fasque at the age of 65 with his wife and three children, Thomas, William and Helen. It was of course William (W E Gladstone) who is undoubtedly Fasque's most famous son; a major political figure and four times Prime Minister to Queen Victoria between 1868 and 1894. William loved Fasque and whenever the rigours of parliamentary life allowed, he would return here where he particularly enjoyed rough shooting, long walks and, perhaps more significantly for the house, compiling the fantastic library that remains intact today.

The house was then lived in for exactly 100 years until, between the First and Second World Wars, it was left for warmer, smaller and more comfortable (less Victorian) residences.

Fasque is now open, by arrangement only, to the public, for we also have a large number of weddings and other functions here during the summer. The amazing thing about the house is how it has remained virtually unchanged since the 1820s. It is perhaps one of the last great Victorian time capsules left in Britain. My uncle's widow still lives in an apartment at one end of the house and the curator's family live in an apartment at the other. The house remains alive and we are very proud of our ability to maintain it in such good condition.

Floors Castle

Kelso, Roxburghshire

Floors Castle, situated in the heart of the Scottish Borders overlooking the River Tweed and Cheviot Hills, has been home to my family since the house was built for the 1st Duke of Roxburghe in 1721. It was designed by William Adam who was both master builder and architect. The 6th Duke embellished the plain Adam features of the building and between 1837 - 1847 the architect William Playfair, drawing his inspiration from the highly ornamented picturesque style of Heriot's Hospital in Edinburgh and letting his imagination and talent run riot, transformed the Castle, creating a roofscape of turrets, pinnacles and cupolas.

Early in the 20th century the 8th Duke married May Goelet, a beautiful young American heiress, who brought to Floors her outstanding collection of fine art. Several of the rooms were altered in the 1920s, including the Drawing Room and Ballroom, and refitted to display a set of Brussels tapestries and the Gobelin tapestries. The apartments now display an outstanding collection of French 17th and 18th century furniture, Chinese and European porcelain, and many other fine works of art.

Like any family home Floors is continuing to undergo change, with rearrangement of furniture, new decoration and additions from time to time. Ultimately it is our family home and we hope that its evolution to meet the needs of continued occupation actually contributes to its interest, warmth and charm.

The Castle is the focus of Roxburghe Estates, an agricultural and sporting estate extending to 56,000 acres. We first opened the Castle to the public in 1977, since then tourism has become an important part of estate business. In 1982 Sunlaws House, a country house on the estate, was converted into a luxury hotel, now known as The Roxburghe. Our latest venture has been to build an 18-hole championship golf course in the grounds of the hotel which was opened in 1997. I am delighted that it has already been recognised as one of the finest inland courses in Scotland and is now home to the Scottish Seniors Open. This is particularly exciting for all of us and gives a great boost to the Borders.

Roxburghe

Fonmon Castle

Barry, South Glamorgan

The family historians have always claimed that Boothbys came over from Denmark in 842; certainly we were in Lincolnshire by 870. Over the millennia, the men of the family have made fortuitous marriages to female relations of the nobility and gentry. From Hereward the Wake in the 11th century, via the Brooke family in the 17th, to the Joneses of Fonmon in the 20th, this has proved a reliable method of acquiring and residing in fine houses. As romantics, eccentrics (seriously so since the 10th Baronet married his first cousin), clerics, gamblers and gifted, if doubtful, politicians, we then fritter it away until the next profitable liaison.

Despite also being of considerable antiquity (started around 1180), Fonmon has only ever belonged to two families. For this reason it lays claim to being the oldest continuously inhabited castle in Wales. The original builders were the St John's, Norman knights, whose ancestor was in charge of William the Conqueror's baggage train.

Fonmon changed hands for the only time in its 800 year history when Sir John St John, in financial difficulties, sold it to Colonel Philip Jones, my direct ancestor, in 1656, during the English Civil War. Colonel Philip was a member of Lord Protector Cromwell's 'Council of Nine', and his influence can be gauged from the Parliamentary record, which records an outraged Member complaining "*We cannot longer have this country ruled from a small castle in Wales*". Not until David Lloyd George, would a Welshman again have such power at the heart of Westminster government.

Despite being impeached at the Restoration (acquitted!), Colonel Philip survived with his fortune intact. The Joneses then provided the usual clutch of public figures including an Admiral who did well by first winning a medal at the Relief of Lucknow, and then another at the sack of Peking, neither of which are noted amongst Britain's most famous naval engagements. Finally, the Joneses ran out of boys and a grand-daughter married my grandfather in the time-honoured manner.

The Castle itself has features from most periods, but the jewel is the 18th century Rococo Library created by Robert Jones III out of the original first floor hall. The contents include fine paintings from both the Boothby and Jones collections.

As the current custodians, my family and I take enormous pleasure in welcoming visitors to share the enjoyment of this proud Saxon-Norman-Welsh heritage.

Sir Brooke Boothby Bt

Glamis Castle

Forfar, Angus

The story of the Castle goes back to 1372 when King Robert II granted Sir John Lyon the Thaneage of Glamis for services rendered to the Crown. In 1376, Sir John married the King's daughter, Princess Joanna, so the royal connection with Glamis goes back long before it became the childhood home of my late, great aunt, the Queen Mother, and the birthplace of Princess Margaret.

Visitors approaching the Castle often draw breath at the sheer magnificence of the building. With the Grampian Mountains providing a spectacular backdrop and the landscaped grounds enhancing the wonderful setting, one can see that the Castle is truly inspiring. It is no surprise, therefore, to learn that it inspired 'Macbeth'.

Like many castles, Glamis has been added to and altered over the years to satisfy the needs and aspirations of succeeding generations and to suit the architectural fashions of the day.

The Castle rooms contain a rich variety of furnishings, tapestries and works of art; highlights include the Victorian Dining Room, which was designed in 1851 - 53. Adjoining the Dining Room is the Crypt where, in the 15th century, the servants would eat and sleep. This room is also thought to contain the 'secret chamber' where, according to legend, an ancestor and his friend were bricked up for having played cards with the Devil on the Sabbath. The Great Hall or Drawing Room, in contrast to the Crypt, is a perfect example of the elegance introduced in the 17th century with many fine paintings, furniture and a beautiful plasterwork ceiling.

There can be few small private chapels in Europe that can match the beauty of the one found in the Castle. It was here that the Old Chevalier, the father of Bonnie Prince Charlie, touched for the 'King's Evil' at the end of the 1715 Jacobite Rebellion. The richly decorated panels on the ceiling show scenes from the life of Christ and the wall paintings show the 12 Apostles.

The Royal Apartments are unique in that they constitute a suite of rooms arranged by the 13th Countess of Strathmore following the marriage of her daughter, Lady Elizabeth Bowes Lyon, into the Royal Family in 1923.

Glamis is a very special place and today remains a much-loved family home to me, my wife Isobel and our three sons.

Strathmore

The Earl of Strathmore & Kinghorne

Glynde Place

Lewes, East Sussex

Glynde Place, built in 1569, has been the home of the family who built it since that date, but on two separate occasions, in 1679 and 1824, it was a cousin with a different name that succeeded. The three families were the Morleys, Trevors (later Viscounts Hampden) and the Brands (later Viscounts Hampden and Barons Dacre).

Each family produced a notable figure. Colonel Harbert Morley, dubbed 'the crooked rebel of Sussex' for his harsh treatment of priests loyal to the Crown, was the leading Parliamentarian in Sussex during the English Civil War. His dislike of the arbitrary rule of Oliver Cromwell caused him to retire during the Commonwealth but he returned to public life on Cromwell's death.

In the middle of the 18th century, Glynde was occupied by Richard Trevor, Bishop of Durham, known as the 'beauty of holiness' by George II. The Bishop transformed Glynde Place by adding a stable block with a clock tower and rebuilding the parish church which is almost in the curtilage of the house, in a Palladian style.

In the 19th century the house was owned by Henry Bouverie Brand, Chief Whip and then Speaker of the House of Commons from 1872-84. He still holds the record for presiding over the longest continual sitting of the House whilst debating the Irish question in 1881: 41 ½ hours. Earlier, Brand was Private Secretary to the Home Secretary during the Chartist riots of 1848, and letters to his wife during that time make vivid reading. The library at Glynde is entirely furnished with his memorabilia.

Glynde is built of Sussex flint and Caen stone around a courtyard which is now an attractive garden. In the Gallery, elegantly panelled by the Bishop, are a large number of portraits of the Trevor family. There is also a fine collection of Italian Old Masters collected by Thomas Brand in the 18th century, including pictures by Guardi, Canaletto, Zuccarelli and Battoni. The furniture is mainly Georgian, but in the Gallery is a fine silver entablature crafted by Garrard, which was given to Henry Brand on his retirement as Government Chief Whip.

I inherited Glynde from my cousin in 1978. My great great grandfather was Mr Speaker Brand and I am also a direct descendant of John Hampden of Shipmoney fame through the marriage of his daughter Ruth to John Trevor. My son Francis, born in 1970, is the heir.

Hampden

Haddon Hall

Bakewell, Derbyshire

Sitting on a limestone outcrop surrounded by gently sloping countryside, Haddon Hall looks like the archetypal picturesque castle and has given rise to many romantic stories. The most famous of these is the tale of Dorothy Vernon's elopement with her suitor, the dashing Sir John Manners in 1563 which caught the Victorian imagination.

A dwelling on the site of the Hall is mentioned for the first time in 1087 in the Domesday Book, and Haddon's architectural history stretches from Norman times to the 17th century. Haddon Hall was never granted full fortress status, but it is nonetheless a fine example of a semi-fortified house.

Haddon Hall has been owned by four principal families: the Peverels (1087 - 1153), the Avenels (1153 - 1170), the Vernons (1170 - 1567) and the Manners (1567 to the present day). The Hall was, and remains, the centrepiece of the surrounding estate, which has fluctuated in size over the centuries, stretching at one stage almost to Sheffield and including most of Bakewell. The estate, though much smaller today, still includes the village of Alport, and part of Rowsley, together with the site of the medieval village of Nether Haddon.

Among the fine features of the Hall are the medieval Banqueting Hall which dates from the 14th century, the Tudor Kitchen and the stunning 16th century Long Gallery which, at 110' long, boasts a beautiful set of bombé (undulating) glass windows which create a glorious play of light on the delicately carved panelling. In the Kitchen the passage of time can be seen in the deeply worn worktops and chopping blocks which have had inches cleaved out of them over the centuries. Other original features such as the mammoth fireplace with spit, salting trough, ovens and sinks also stand as reminders of the variety of jobs that were carried out in a busy Tudor kitchen.

Untouched and uninhabited for 200 years, the Hall bypassed the 18th and 19th century alterations common to so many other country houses, and so remains one of the finest examples of architecture from the Medieval and Tudor periods. It is also famed for its garden which is one of the most beautiful examples of English Renaissance design.

Haddon's restoration and transformation to near its present condition was begun by my grandfather, the 9th Duke of Rutland, at the beginning of the 20th century – work and care which I am pleased to continue today.

Hamptworth Lodge

Salisbury, Wiltshire

Nigel Anderson

It is thought the first house was built on this site in about 1620. In the years that followed it was altered greatly and then finally demolished by my maternal grandfather, H C Moffatt, who inherited in 1900. The house passed into my mother's family c1860 and then to Moffatt via his uncle, George Morrison, who made it over to his nephew, H C Cumberbach. I inherited Hamptworth in 1952.

My grandfather had always wanted to build a Jacobean/Elizabethan style house to hold his collection of furniture of that period. On coming down from Oxford, his father suggested he should join him in the City, but this held little appeal for Moffatt who was a countryman at heart and keen to "do something with his hands". He apprenticed himself to Tims, the boat builders in Oxford, in order to learn the art of woodworking. A man of many talents, he was an accomplished organist, an authority on silver and knowledgeable about the iron and lead work contained in Elizabethan houses. He was also an excellent shot and fisherman.

Moffatt started to make furniture in about 1904 and continued, in particular his woodcarving and design, until old age finally caught up with him in 1945. The majority of his pieces, all made from English hardwoods, remain in the house still, in addition to furniture collected by him during his lifetime. In 1956, death duties forced us to sell a large number of pictures and other artefacts from the house but we managed, against all the odds, to keep the Moffatt collection virtually intact.

The garden at Hamptworth is laid out in the Elizabethan style, the main lawn being the exact length of archery practice distance for "the national service men" of the time. Many interesting varieties of trees grow in the area surrounding the house and garden. Unusually for Wiltshire, the soil on the estate is sandy and acid dictating that, of necessity, we must be foresters rather than farmers. Timber – mixed broadleaf and conifer – is grown as a crop, the production of which supports the house, our home, which is occupied by my wife and myself.

N. Anderson

Nigel Anderson

Hergest Croft Gardens

Kington, Herefordshire

Lawrence Banks

Hergest Croft Gardens were begun in 1896 by William Hartland Banks and his wife Dorothy on land owned by the family since 1840. William, a banker, traveller and photographer, also had a passion for gardening and plant collecting. He modelled the gardens on the principles of William Robinson as set out in his book 'The English Flower Garden' and the area around the house especially reflects his emphasis on natural planting. Many of the earliest plantings come from the collections of Ernest 'Chinese' Wilson for the famous nursery firm of Veitch. One of the great trees dating from this era is a huge *Davidia involucrata*, the Pocket-handkerchief or Dove tree, with masses of white flowers in May.

The Gardens have since been developed by his son Dick and his wives Jane and Rosamund and are now cared for by myself, William's grandson, and my wife Elizabeth. The female influence at Hergest Croft has been considerable – Dorothy Banks was brought up in a family with strong connections to the Arts & Crafts movement, Rosamund was the founder of the London florists, Pullbrook & Gould, and Elizabeth is one of Britain's leading landscape architects.

The woodland garden in Park Wood developed after the First World War, with extensive plantings of rhododendrons, some of which are now over 30 feet tall. This has been described as '*the nearest thing to a Himalayan valley in England*'. The parkland around the garden is planted with groups of exotic trees merging imperceptibly into the Herefordshire countryside. The huge range of trees and shrubs, which have been added to continuously by Dick and myself, is '*one of the finest collections of woody plants in private hands*'. Many of the new introductions from plant collectors in China since 1980 have been planted in the Maple Grove started in the 1980s.

Hergest Croft is much more than an arboretum. There is an old-fashioned Kitchen Garden graced by some of Elizabeth's designs for the Chelsea Flower Show, spring borders under an ancient apple avenue and twin herbaceous borders. Above all, however, this is a family garden reflecting the interests and enthusiasms of the succeeding generations of Banks and it continues to be developed today.

Lawrence Banks

Lawrence Banks

Hever Castle

Edenbridge, Kent

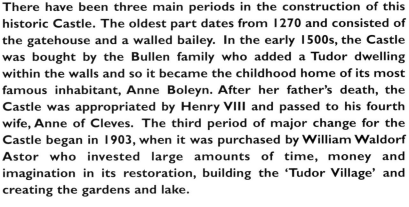

There have been three main periods in the construction of this historic Castle. The oldest part dates from 1270 and consisted of the gatehouse and a walled bailey. In the early 1500s, the Castle was bought by the Bullen family who added a Tudor dwelling within the walls and so it became the childhood home of its most famous inhabitant, Anne Boleyn. After her father's death, the Castle was appropriated by Henry VIII and passed to his fourth wife, Anne of Cleves. The third period of major change for the Castle began in 1903, when it was purchased by William Waldorf Astor who invested large amounts of time, money and imagination in its restoration, building the 'Tudor Village' and creating the gardens and lake.

The award-winning gardens, which we continue to maintain to a high standard today, were mainly laid out between 1904 and 1908 by Joseph Cheal and Son for William Waldorf Astor. The Italian Garden houses a stunning collection of Roman statuary and the Tudor Gardens include a yew hedge maze. The walled Rose Garden and the 110 metre herbaceous border are other major features. Recent additions include the exciting splashing Water Maze on Sixteen Acre Island which challenges adults and children alike to reach a folly located in the centre of a large circular pond, without getting wet. The Sunday Walk Garden, set either side of a woodland walk alongside a stream, was opened in 2001.

As the present owner, I acquired Hever Castle in 1983 through my company Broadland Properties Ltd. Today, the homely atmosphere of the Castle houses historic 16th century portraits, furniture and tapestries, many of which reflect a diligent search by Astor for *objets d'art* suitable for the restored Castle. Other artefacts include two magnificent Books of Hours (prayer books), both signed and inscribed by Anne Boleyn. The newly presented Council Chamber in the 13th century gatehouse contains recently acquired swords and armour which have been added to the existing collections of historic instruments of execution, torture and discipline.

John Guthrie

Highclere Castle

Hampshire

Highclere Castle stands on the foundations of an earlier house built on the site of the medieval palace of the Bishops of Winchester. After the Reformation, Highclere was owned successively by the Fitzwilliam, Kingsmill and Lucy families. In 1679, it was bought by Sir Robert Sawyer, Attorney General to Charles II and James II, and bequeathed to his daughter who, by her marriage to the Earl of Pembroke, brought Highclere to the Herbert family. At her death, the house and estate passed to her second son and then to his nephew who was created 1st Earl of Carnarvon by a grateful George III.

The present house was designed by Sir Charles Barry, commissioned by the 3rd Earl to transform the plain Georgian house he had inherited into a grand mansion which would impress the world. Barry called it Anglo-Italian and much preferred it to the Houses of Parliament which he was building at the same time. The 3rd Earl was never to see the completion of the remodelling – he died in 1850 leaving his son, the 4th Earl to finish the interiors.

Paintings by Gainsborough, Reynolds, van Dyck and family portraits by Sir William Beechey adorn the walls of each room. The furniture throughout the Castle is a blend of English and European styles. In the Library there is an ornate desk and chair made for Napoleon Bonaparte and acquired by the 3rd Earl in 1827.

The Herberts have distinguished themselves particularly in three spheres: politics, travel and horseracing.

Politics: In 1780 Henry Herbert diffused a tense situation during the Gordon riots, the 2nd Earl vociferously opposed the Reform Bill in 1832, and the 3rd Earl the Repeal of the Corn Laws. The 4th Earl was Secretary of State for the Colonies and Lord Lieutenant of Ireland. My father, the 7th Earl, was tireless in his work for the Hampshire County Council, the South East Regional Planning Authority and several All-Party committees.

Travel: The 3rd, 4th and 5th Earls travelled extensively throughout the world and the 5th Earl's interest in Egyptology led him, with Howard Carter, to discover the tomb of Tutankhamun.

Horseracing: The Highclere Stud was founded by the 5th Earl and the 1930 Derby winner, Blenheim, was bred by the 6th Earl. The 7th Earl, my father, became the Queen's Racing Manager. Today my brother, Harry Herbert, my sister, Carolyn Warren, and I are all involved with the farms and the Stud.

Hoghton Tower

Preston, Lancashire

Perched 600 feet above sea level, looking more like a medieval hilltop village or an ancient castle, broods Hoghton Tower, the third building to occupy Hoghton hill since 1080. It is a striking location and commands extensive views over the Lancashire plains. The present house, rebuilt by Thomas de Hoghton between 1560 and 1565, has retained its Tudor Elizabethan character and construction.

The house is reached by a long straight avenue and is built around the classic design of having an Inner and an Outer Courtyard. No additions have been made since 1565, though its medieval Keep was destroyed in the Civil War and its pre-Reformation chapel allowed to decay. During the latter half of the 19th century an extensive but sympathetic restoration was accomplished, but neither of the two lost buildings were rebuilt. Its style is somewhat medieval but its embellishments and outlook clearly reflect the Renaissance.

Hoghton has hosted the 'comings and goings' of many varied guests and visitors. The most glittering occasion the house has hosted was in August 1617, with the arrival of King James I. The Hoghtons lavished hospitality and entertainment on the King and his Court for three whole days, and whilst here, the loin of beef was knighted 'Sir Loin' and the 'Book of Sports' was signed.

'Men of Destiny', Edmund Campion SJ, Bonnie Prince Charlie and John Wesley left their mark here, whilst Turner, A Devis and Geo Cattermole have painted from it; Ben Johnson, Weever, Inigo Jones have all written of the house's family and Ainsworth and Dickens have concocted colourful fiction about it.

The family also has not lacked characters or contributors to national life, Thomas de Hoghton choosing to leave his newly-built house for voluntary exile rather than changing religion; the first two baronets siding with the Royalist cause whilst their sons and descendants choosing Parliament for the next 200 years. Beyond those responsibilities the family never lost its origins of military service, culminating with my late father, Sir Cuthbert de Hoghton, helping to create the Royal Naval Air Service. Losing £300,000 in Confederate Bonds was, even in its time, considered a real fortune but 30 years earlier Sir Henry de Hoghton's grandfather, Sir Henry Philip, had gambled and lost Liverpool.

Hoghton was my childhood home and holds many happy memories. Being part of the landscape gives a real sense of timelessness and solidity but it is *men not walls* that make a house strong, hence we hope that our current endeavours can keep a house on this hill for many years to come.

Holker Hall

Grange-over-Sands, Cumbria

Holker is a Norse word which can be translated as 'a rising in marshy land'. Although the origins are lost in the mists of time, the earliest records of a house on the present site date back to the beginning of the 16th century. It is set in exceptionally beautiful countryside, gardens merging into parkland, with hills on one side and the expanse of Morecambe Bay on the other.

Always inherited and never sold, Holker has been home to three families; the Prestons, Lowthers and Cavendishes, each generation making its mark, either through altering the landscape or changing the house by adding, refacing, embellishing and even rebuilding, as was necessary after the disastrous fire of 1871.

The fire destroyed the entire west wing, including numerous paintings, pieces of furniture, statues, portraits and valuable books. Undaunted by this catastrophe, William Cavendish, the 7th Duke of Devonshire, began plans to rebuild the west wing on an even grander scale, and employed the architects Paley and Austin. Built in red sandstone, it covered the same site as the previous wing, and despite its emulation of Elizabethan architecture, it remains unmistakably Victorian. It is a marvellous reflection of its age with its atmosphere of confidence, spaciousness and prosperity.

Holker has always been loved by its owners. The 7th Duke preferred it to any of his other properties and, in 1908 when the house was left to my grandfather, and not to his elder brother Victor, the Duke muttered bitterly *'Holker, the best loved house in England'*. He and his family left in tears, with a photograph to record the occasion.

One of the greatest joys of Holker is the garden and I am indebted to the generations of keen, enthusiastic and gifted gardeners for the wonderful collection of trees and shrubs. There are trees surviving at Holker suggesting that my ancestors had an interest in collecting unusual trees as early as the 1750s.

The record reveals that my ancestors felt that for them *'Holker was more desirable, more favoured by Providence and more enhanced with natural beauty than any other place on earth'*. I hope our visitors will feel as welcome today as would the family relations and friends arriving at Holker 100 years ago.

Cavendish of Furness

The Lord Cavendish of Furness DL

Holkham Hall

Wells-next-the-Sea, Norfolk

Sir Edward Coke (1552 - 1634) founded the family fortune which, in turn, enabled Thomas Coke, the 1st Earl of Leicester, to build Holkham Hall in 1734. Sir Edward, Attorney General to Queen Elizabeth I and Chief Justice to James I, was the most brilliant lawyer of his time. He was able, so the story goes, to digest even the most complicated parts of English law and chose an ostrich as the family's crest – the birds are reputed to have an iron digestion.

Holkham Hall itself was not built until five generations later, when Thomas Coke (1697 - 1759) returned from his Grand Tour of Italy, along with considerable quantities of antiquities and treasures. It soon became obvious that the medieval house on the site was too small to house such a great collection and so the Hall we see today was gradually conceived. Designed by William Kent and Lord Burlington, whom Thomas had met during his Tour, and Coke himself, the Hall is one of the finest examples of Palladian architecture in the country.

Three years after Thomas Coke's death in 1762, Holkham Hall was eventually completed and it is thanks to his widow, Lady Margaret Tufton, that the interiors were finally finished in accordance with her husband's wishes. He left copious instructions as to where each painting, sculpture or piece of furniture was to be placed, all recorded in the inventory of 1773. We still possess those records today and it is an on-going project of mine to restore the house and its contents to how Thomas originally intended it should look.

The great estate then passed, in 1776, to Thomas William Coke who was to become the 1st Earl of Leicester of the second creation. An MP for more than 50 years, Thomas was known as 'Coke of Norfolk' and highly regarded for his ideas and patronage of agriculture, which ushered in sweeping improvements across the land.

Holkham, still privately owned, is the centre of a 25,000 acre agricultural Estate providing funds and resources which maintain not only the house, but also ensure that the social fabric of rural life remains intact. In recent times, our enterprises have expanded to include a caravan park, a building company and an hotel. More than 160 people are now employed on the Estate and we are constantly looking for ways in which to enhance our businesses in order to ensure that it continues to prosper. The house is therefore not a stuffy museum but part of a thriving community in which my family and I, along with many others, all live and work.

Edward Leicester

Hopetoun House

South Queensferry, West Lothian

As an architectural paradigm of the first half of the 18th century, Hopetoun House is unique in Scotland. Built for the Hope family, it combines in one building the talents of Scotland's most influential architects of that era, Sir William Bruce and the outstanding Adam family – William and his sons, John and Robert.

Hopetoun, in its original form, reflected Bruce's interests in Italian and French sources. As an example of French influence on British 18th century architecture, Hopetoun is notable. The Adam façade that later masked the Bruce house and replaced his Italianate colonnades is, with the loss of Hamilton Palace, the most palatial in Scotland. Adaptations undertaken by James Gillespie Graham in the early 19th century were unusual, since the historic interiors were, for the most part, retained while upgrading them to establish a parade of rooms that, for metropolitan, even regal, grandeur, are unique in Scotland.

Among the interiors created by the Adam family was a range of state apartments with glorious gilded ceilings and specially made furniture; magnificent examples being the State bed and a pair of Cullen commodes. It was here that Hopetoun welcomed its most distinguished visitor during the next century. In August 1822, King George IV paid a visit as part of his State journey to Scotland. The grounds of Hopetoun were thrown open to local residents, guards of honour filled the courtyard and the new monarch was received at 1.15pm by the 4th Earl and his family. Following a light and, by all accounts, somewhat subdued (some turtle soup and three glasses of wine) lunch, the King left at three o'clock to board the Royal Yacht at Port Edgar.

The grounds at Hopetoun are the most outstanding example of landscape design in the grand manner remaining largely intact in Scotland. The relationship between the house, its landscape setting and pre-existing features of the countryside is one of the earliest and best examples of Formalism in Scotland, conceived to create an integrated design composition of grand proportion.

Hopetoun has been the home of my family ever since it was built. In 1974 a charitable trust was established to own and preserve the house with its historic contents and surrounding landscape for the benefit of the public for all time. My family, however, continue to live in the private side of the house and it remains very much home to us.

Linlithgow

The Marquess of Linlithgow

Houghton Hall

King's Lynn, Norfolk

Built by Sir Robert Walpole in 1720-27, Houghton is the epitome of Palladian splendour. Sir Robert was First Minister under both George I and George II and every detail was intended to reflect his increasing power and influence, as well as his taste (although many contemporaries found the house absurdly grandiose). Houghton was the first large house in Norfolk to be faced with stone, which was shipped by sea from Whitby in Yorkshire to King's Lynn.

The original plans by Colen Campbell were much modified by James Gibbs, who probably suggested the four corner cupolas, and by Thomas Ripley. The interiors were designed and executed by William Kent from about 1725-34, and Kent may also have been responsible for the Stable Block, built in brick and Norfolk Carr stone.

Sir Robert died in 1745 leaving enormous debts, and Houghton gradually fell into disrepair. His grandson, the feckless and dissolute 3rd Earl of Orford, sold the famous collection of pictures to the Empress Catherine of Russia, and later lost the great outside staircases in a wager (in 1974 my grandmother had the staircase on the West Front replaced, using stone from the original quarry in Yorkshire). The 3rd Earl lived in only a fraction of the house and spent much of his time coursing hares and racing at Newmarket. He was prone to fits of madness, but lived to a good age at Houghton with his mistress, Patty Turk.

The 4th Earl of Cholmondeley, whose grandfather had married Sir Robert's daughter Mary, inherited Houghton in 1797 (from Horace Walpole) but only lived there a few years before moving back to the family's base in Cheshire.

My grandparents, Sybil and 'Rock' (the 5th Marquess) came to Houghton after the First World War, and at once set about resuscitating both the house and the estate. My grandfather died in 1967 and the house was first opened to the public a few years later. The Picture Gallery was made into a museum to house my father's collection of 20,000 model soldiers and this proved as much of a draw as the house itself.

When I took over the running of the house in 1990, I started a programme of repair and restoration, including re-plumbing and rewiring. In 1996 we opened the Walled Gardens, replanted in memory of my grandmother and, in 2000, a long vanished 1200 foot ha-ha was replaced at the end of the lawn. Other recent plans include the reinstatement of hedges and avenues on the West Front, and the integration of contemporary art works in the park and grounds. I believe it is projects like these which help to keep old houses alive and vibrant.

David Cholmondeley

The Marquess of Cholmondeley

Hutton-in-the-Forest

Penrith, Cumbria

Possibly the earliest mention of Hutton-in-the-Forest is in the Arthurian legend when Sir Gawain rode *'into a deep forest, that was wonderfully wild, with high hills on every side'* in search of the Green Knight and, having met him at the Green Chapel, they rode on to the Knight's 'Castle of Hutton'. Certainly, the house was one of the main manors in the great Royal Forest of Inglewood, which stretched from Penrith to Carlisle.

Only one pele tower survives of the medieval stronghold which the Fletchers, rich merchants from Cockermouth who later married the Vanes, bought from the de Hoton family in 1605. They set about converting the castle into a country house by filling in the moat and building a fine gallery over an open arcade. The house provides an interesting journey through English architectural history as succeeding generations have altered and added to it. No one has had the will or the wealth to re-do the entire house, although designs were drawn up in the 1840s to remodel the courtyard front. These plans were never carried out and it is still very recognisable as the house in Kip's view of 1705.

The interiors of the house are as varied in date and style as the exteriors. Two favourite features are the 17th century Cupid Staircase, carved with the fattest of cherubs playing amongst acanthus leaves and the delicate rococo plaster ceiling of the Cupid Room. We have added a contemporary chandelier, ceramics and pictures to the collection, which is notable for its English furniture and portraits.

There is still much to be done to the gardens. We are lucky in having the grey-pink stone of the house and a variety of magnificent trees as a backdrop. The Walled Garden is now a flower garden, mainly herbaceous and, at its best, most beautiful. The Victorian Low Garden below the South Terrace is hardly under control and the 18th century lake neglected. We hope to restore them before too long, but it is a major challenge.

Principally, Hutton is our home. We take pleasure in having visitors who enjoy coming here but most importantly, we hope that one of our children will want to carry on living here which will make it all worthwhile.

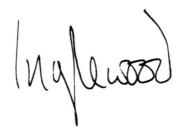

The Lord Inglewood

Inveraray Castle

Inveraray, Argyll

Inveraray has been home to my family for around 600 years. Sir Duncan Campbell moved his headquarters from Innis Chonnell Castle on Loch Awe to a fortified tower house – befitting the troubled times that the people of Scotland still endured – which he built a short distance to the north of the present Castle. During the reigns of the 7th, 8th and 9th Earls in the 16th and 17th centuries, the grounds were enhanced with much tree planting and the creation of avenues and vistas, many of which exist to this day and the Policies are some of the best preserved early landscape work in Scotland.

When my ancestor the 3rd Duke – his father the 10th Earl was created 1st Duke in 1701 – inherited the title from his brother in 1743, the old Castle was in a serious state of decay. A contemporary report states that there were *'few parts of it Sufficient. There are large Rents in both side Walls'*. In spite of his relatively advanced age, he resolved to build an entirely new home to a totally different design. He engaged Roger Morris, a London architect, and within two years, building had commenced. Part of Duke Archibald's "Grand Conception" included a decision to relocate the Old Town of Inveraray. And so began in 1751 one of the most ambitious building projects ever undertaken in the Highlands, and what you see today is indubitably one of the best preserved planned towns in Scotland.

The interiors of the house were designed by Robert Mylne under the instruction of the 5th Duke and work was completed about 1790. The superb Armoury Hall with its stunning collection of contemporary arms links the building to its fortified keep predecessor, whereas the beautiful drawing room with its French tapestries and fine furniture, much of it the work of Edinburgh craftsmen, reflects the more sumptuous style of living 18th century gentlemen had come to enjoy.

I am understandably proud of the achievements of my predecessors and, with my wife, Eleanor, commend Inveraray Castle to visitors. We endorse the words of James Hogg written following a visit in 1803 *"But the greatest beauty of all is this: the closer the inspections the more exalted your admiration; and the better your acquaintance the greater your esteem"*.

The Duke of Argyll

Kentwell Hall

Long Melford, Suffolk

Patrick Phillips

Approached by an ancient avenue of limes almost a mile long, Kentwell Hall emerges intriguingly out of the distance in all its beauty. This initial impression is reinforced when you get closer to the house. Warm red brick in a myriad of hues, countless leaded light panes in numerous windows and the cream dressings reflect all light conditions. This impression is enhanced by the brick-lined moats which reflect shimmering images of the buildings.

Architecturally the house stands at the crossroads between a medieval hall house, which the Centre Block in the early 16th century represents, and the Elizabethan E-Plan which, after the additions of the wings, it appears to epitomise. Yet it was finished well before Elizabeth came to the throne. The house was begun in about 1500 by the Clopton family, long powerful in East Anglia and responsible for rebuilding Melford's incomparable Parish Church. Building seems to have proceeded over several decades under Sir William Clopton (d 1530) and then his son Thomas. In 1626 the house passed by marriage into the D'Ewes families and later the D'Arcys, and was bought in 1676, by Sir Thomas Robinson Bt who planted the magnificent lime avenue. It remained substantially unaltered, while families came and went, until the 1820s when the architect Thomas Hopper, engaged by the new owner, Robert Hart Logan, remodelled much of the interior in a varied Gothick taste. Sadly, Logan was not to enjoy the house for long and following his untimely death in 1838, soon after he became an MP, Kentwell was sold to Edward Starkie Bence.

When Starkie Bence died, his son let the house for 50 years to a succession of tenants until it was requisitioned for accommodation in World War II. By the time I first saw Kentwell, one July day in 1970, it had suffered nearly 100 years of neglect and was in a serious state of decay. I saw the condition of the house as an attraction not a deterrent. Ever since works, from restoration to new building, have continued uninterrupted, with just as much effort expended upon recreating and developing Kentwell's once fine gardens.

The fact that the house is a home is evident to any visitor. There are no grand State Rooms. Every room is eminently inhabitable and usually boasts signs of current occupation, if not clutter. We are very lucky to be at Kentwell. We are here by choice and have made it our own. We feel more like the original builders must have felt rather than living in someone else's house.

Patrick Phillips

Patrick Phillips

Layer Marney Tower

Colchester, Essex

Nicholas Charrington

Built in the first half of Henry VIII's reign, Layer Marney Tower is the apotheosis of the Tudor gatehouse. The building is principally the creation of Henry, 1st Lord Marney, who died in 1523. His son John continued the building work but died just two years later, leaving no male heirs to continue the family line, or the construction. What was completed was the main range measuring some 300' long, the principal gatehouse that is about 80' tall, a fine array of outbuildings, and a new church. In building on this scale the Marneys were following the example of their monarch, Henry VIII, who believed that a building should reflect the magnificence of its owner.

After the death of John Marney, the house passed to Sir Brian Tuke. His widowed daughter-in-law entertained Queen Elizabeth I for two days in 1579, most probably staying in what is now the billiard room on the first floor of the gatehouse. The house has passed through many different families over the last five centuries, some staying for a few years, others for several generations.

The buildings suffered considerable damage from the 'Great Earthquake' of 1884, and a subsequent report in 'The Builder' stated 'the outlay needed to restore the towers to anything like a sound and habitable condition would be so large that the chance of the work ever being done appears remote indeed'. Repairs were begun by the Peache family, who re-floored and re-roofed the gatehouse, as well as creating the garden to the south.

Walter de Zoete carried on the repairs and alterations, enlarging the gardens, building a folly known as the Tea House and converting the stables into a Long Gallery where he housed his collection of furniture, paintings and objets d'art.

When the house came up for sale in 1959, my father had a staff job with the Trucial Oman Scouts in Aden and my mother had planned to visit him. He was called elsewhere for a few days, prompting a telegraph from my mother 'if you go to Sharjah, I shall buy Layer Marney'. He went and she bought.

With the help of what is now English Heritage, they embarked on a programme of repairs, principally to the terracotta windows, chimneys and parts of the roof. In 1989 they moved to a smaller, warmer house, and Sheila and I moved in. We now have four children, and I can think of no better place for us to be.

Nicholas Charrington

Nicholas Charrington

Leeds Castle

Maidstone, Kent

The name 'Leeds' derives from two Anglo-Saxon words meaning a settlement above a stream such as the village of Leeds is. The Castle was founded circa 1120 by Robert de Crèvecœur. His descendants continued to live there until around 1260 when, following a mistake over a matter of loyalty, Leeds came into the possession of Edward I and his wife, Eleanor of Castile.

For the next 300 years Leeds remained a royal home. Henry VIII made major improvements to the Castle and his son, Edward VI, finally gave it away to one of his statesmen, Sir Anthony St Leger KG. It later passed into the ownership of the famous Culpeper and Fairfax families. The Castle's fortunes varied between the 16th and 19th centuries; at one time a prison, it was damaged by fire, Gothicised and then returned to its medieval appearance. In 1926 the wealthy Anglo-American heiress, Olive Wilson Filmer, later Lady Baillie, bought it. She was the daughter of Pauline Whitney, a favourite at the White House during the Cleveland administration, and the British aristocrat Almeric Paget, later Lord Queenborough.

Lady Baillie devoted the rest of her life, and a considerable fortune, to restoring the historic buildings in a bid to create a country house for social gatherings and, most importantly, a family home. A society hostess, she brought European royalty, politicians and stars of stage and screen to Leeds, introducing golf, croquet, film and even the first outdoor heated swimming pool in the country, for their entertainment.

A keen collector of art and antiques, Lady Baillie drew on the best architects and artistic advisers in Europe and America, including Armand-Albert Rateau and Stéphane Boudin. She also indulged her own passion for exotic birds and bought many for the Castle aviary which is today famous for its conservation and breeding programmes for rare and endangered species.

On Lady Baillie's death in 1974, Leeds Castle was bequeathed to a charitable trust to preserve "the loveliest castle in the world" open to the public in perpetuity. The Trust was charged with the task of maintaining Leeds Castle as a living castle and not a stone museum.

Armstrong of Ilminster

Lord Armstrong of Ilminster

Chairman, The Leeds Castle Foundation

Leighton Hall

Carnforth, Lancashire

Richard Gillow Reynolds

Leighton Hall's setting, in a bowl of parkland against the dramatic backdrop of the Lakeland mountains, can deservedly be described as spectacular. Nestling in 1,550 acres of lush grounds on the Lancashire and Cumbria borders, this romantic, Gothic house is the lived-in home of the Gillow Reynolds family. The world famous furniture-making Gillows, and their ancestors, have made their home at Leighton Hall for more than 750 years.

The earliest records of Leighton go back to 1246, when Adam D'Avranches had a fortified manor here. Since then, there have been 26 owners of the property including Sir George Middleton, loyal Cavalier and High Sheriff of Lancashire; Albert Hodgson who was jailed after the Jacobite rebellion of 1715 and the colourful Richard Thomas Gillow, was known throughout Lancashire as the "Old Squire". After D'Avranches' original manor was sacked and burned by government troops following the 1715 Jacobite uprising, Leighton Hall was rebuilt in 1760 in the Adam style by George Towneley.

In 1822, the house was sold to Richard Gillow, grandson of the founder of the Gillow business, who added the striking, Gothic façade, giving Leighton a fashionable grandeur. A new wing was built in 1870 to accommodate the large Victorian household.

Leighton boasts many unusual, unique and early pieces of Gillow furniture: in the Dining Room is an expanding table, thought to be the prototype of this style; in the Drawing Room, overlooking the Lakeland mountains, is an 18th century games table and a pair of early Victorian work tables can be found in the Library. There is also a fine collection of paintings, several magnificent clocks, many *objets d'art* and interesting curiosities, including a lock of King James II's hair.

Leighton's gardens and parkland are the 18th century legacy of George Towneley, although subsequent owners have added their own embellishments such as the Walled Garden and woodland walks.

I live at Leighton with my wife Suzie and our daughters, Katherine and Lucy. Like my Gillow ancestors, we are continuing to improve the Hall and enjoy welcoming our visitors. Thousands of people now visit Leighton annually, enjoying entertaining tours of the house and the beautiful gardens.

R Gillow Reynolds

Levens Hall

Kendal, Cumbria

Levens has been in continual family ownership since the 13th century, only once changing hands, between cousins, in 1688. De Redmans, Bellinghams, Grahmes, Howards and Bagots have all contributed to the estate by developing the house from a primitive pele tower into an Elizabethan mansion, with additions in 1690 and in 1820.

This continuity has brought together not only a fascinating cast of characters, but also personal possessions, furniture, paintings and artefacts which create the Hall's interest and atmosphere. The de Redmans built the pele tower and the medieval core of the house which forms the centre of the present building. James Bellingham created the grand Elizabethan mansion that visitors see today, bringing in the finest craftsmen to carve local oak panelling and Italian plaster workers to embellish the ceilings and walls with coats of arms. His Elizabethan farms are still part of the estate today.

As Privy Purse to King James II, Sir James Grahme was a prominent member of the Stuart Court. Following the King's abdication, he came to live at Levens. He added two wings to the rear of the Hall and filled the house with fine furniture and possessions which remain for visitors to see today. Grahme also brought the King's French gardener, Monsieur Beaumont (whose royal appointment was brought to an abrupt end by the fall of the last Catholic ruler of Britain) to lay out the gardens and park, the design of which remains virtually unchanged. The world-famous topiary garden continues to amaze as much now as it did in Beaumont's day and its preservation in the face of changing fashions over 300 years makes it a unique attraction for visitors.

Mary Howard, James Grahme's great, great granddaughter, was an heiress with four estates and was highly regarded as a local benefactress. As Mary had no children, Levens was bequeathed to her great, great nephew, Josceline Bagot. His grandfather, Sir Charles Bagot, had a distinguished career in the diplomatic service and married a niece of the Duke of Wellington, Lady Mary Wellesley, who bequeathed to Levens many interesting artefacts belonging to Napoleon and Wellington.

We love Levens and hope that our children, who have grown up here, will feel the same as we do, so that the house will be preserved as a family home that visitors can continue to appreciate and enjoy.

Hal Bagot

Longleat

Warminster, Wiltshire

Longleat has been my home for the past 40 years and more, and as I walk its lengthy corridors I am conscious that I have shared it with at least 8 million other pairs of feet – some more famous than others – Elizabeth I, Charles II – some perhaps less so with the thousands of visitors that we receive each year.

The original Longleat was an Augustinian priory founded in the 13th century, but the present house dates from the 1560s when the estate was acquired by Sir John Thynne, following the Dissolution of the Monasteries. Sir John died in 1580 with Longleat still unfinished, though building operations had not deterred Queen Elizabeth I from visiting in 1574 – the first in a long line of royal guests. Longleat is widely regarded as the best example of high Elizabethan architecture in Britain and one of the most beautiful stately homes open to the public. It was my father, the 6th Marquess, who first perceived that a house of this magnitude and splendour could become a major tourist attraction.

Most visitors to Longleat leave with a very distinct reaction to their experience of the House. The quality of the architecture and the setting are universally acclaimed and the interior has something for everyone to enjoy. In fact, Longleat House is a timeless piece of history including artefacts and furnishings from every century since Sir John Thynne commenced building in 1568, to my own murals that I have painted in the West Wing.

Apart from the House, Longleat hosts a multitude of attractions. The Safari Park, a firm favourite with all our visitors, offers face-to-face experiences with some of the world's most magnificent animals living free in a superb parkland setting. Longleat might be famous for its lions but you could also come nose-to-nose with a monkey, tiger or giraffe!

The parkland was landscaped by 'Capability' Brown; there is a wide range of trees and sculptures within the Pleasure Walk and visitors with plenty of energy can take up the challenge of one of the World's Longest Hedge Mazes – Longleat offers something for everyone.

It is my hope that Longleat is a really special place for all generations – a place to explore the beautiful surroundings and learn in a fun way about the natural world and their heritage. It is a place where visitors can bring their children who, in the future, might bring their own children.

Lulworth Castle

Wareham, Dorset

Wilfrid Weld

Lulworth Castle and its estate, which included land granted to the Norman de Newburgh family by Henry I and the monastic lands of Bindon Abbey, was purchased in 1641 by Humphrey Weld from the Earl of Suffolk for £30,000. Humphrey's grandfather, also called Humphrey, had moved to London to seek his fortune at the age of 19. He was apprenticed into the Grocers' Company and went on to become a prosperous merchant. Knighted in 1603, he became Lord Mayor of London in 1609 and following his death a year later, Sir Humphrey left a large fortune to his grandson.

The mansion, Bindon House, was destroyed by fire and the estate badly damaged by occupying Parliamentary troops during the Civil War. This forced Humphrey Weld, on his return from supporting King Charles, to improve and live in the Castle as the family home, which ensured its survival, and to create formal gardens around it.

Little further was done to alter the Castle and its surroundings until Edward Weld, in 1760, promoted an Enclosure Act to remove the village from beside the Castle in order to create a park in the modern fashion. He died before he could make any changes and it was his son, Thomas, the owner from 1777-1810, who was largely responsible, with the help of the architect, John Tasker, for turning Lulworth Castle into a great 18th century mansion. He engaged Richard Woods to landscape the present park and built, with special permission from George III, the nearby Catholic chapel, the first in England to be used for public worship since the Reformation. His eldest son, Thomas, was created a Cardinal in 1830, one of the few Catholics to be married and ordained.

After the castle was virtually destroyed by the disastrous fire in 1929, which burned for three days, the family lived outside the park until, in 1977, the new house was built some 300 metres from the Castle. The Castle has now been restored as a usable building by English Heritage and, together with the Lulworth Castle estate, is owned and managed by the Weld family.

Wilfrid Weld (signature)

Manderston

Duns, Berwickshire

Manderston, built between 1903 and 1905 on the site of the original 18th century house was inherited by my great, great uncle, Sir James Miller, a great sportsman and horse racing enthusiast and one of the most wealthy commoners in the country.

It is a house on which no expense was spared, Sir James Miller telling his architect, John Kinross, when he enquired how much he could spend, that *"it simply didn't matter"*. The result is an elegant Georgian-style mansion that displays every convenience and luxury of the Edwardian age, both indoors and out. Marble from seven different countries and the only silver staircase in the world feature in the house. The state rooms are magnificent, the ballroom in particular being a jewel, with all its original furnishings still intact. Upstairs the bedrooms and bathrooms are truly luxurious and the servants' quarters below stairs show meticulous planning for the staff's convenience. On the night of 7th November 1905, a magnificent ball, the first and last to be given by Sir James and Lady Miller, was held to celebrate the completion of Manderston. Sir James died three months later, aged 42, and the style of life epitomised by the ball and his creation of Manderston was already doomed, overtaken by events worldwide.

The house stands in 56 acres of gardens, comprising terraces in front of the house; formal gardens that are at their best in mid to late summer; lawns with magnificent mature trees; a lake and a woodland garden with an extensive collection of azaleas and rhododendrons, in bloom in May and June. The estate buildings are as luxurious as the house, with an octagonal marble dairy standing at the end of mock cloisters, and stables described as the finest in the world, and often mistaken for the house itself.

Manderston has been used as a film location several times and most recently was '*The Edwardian Country House*' in the Channel 4 series. Visitors are assured of a warm welcome and have the chance to see the sumptuous state rooms along with the domestic offices which were vital to the smooth running of such a house. We are very pleased to welcome visitors to Manderston, which is our home and in which members of our family have lived, almost continually, since 1855.

Palmer

Mannington Hall

Saxthorpe, Norfolk

Mannington Hall was built in 1460 by William Lumnor during the Wars of the Roses – the house's fortifications, moat and battlements being practical as well as ornamental. The Hall was subsequently owned by the Tirel, Dodge and Potts families until the 1740s, when it was bought by Horatio, 1st Lord Walpole, diplomat brother of Sir Robert, regarded as our first Prime Minister.

At nearby Wolterton (see p180), Horatio built his mansion house and intended the Hall at Mannington for his wife on his death, but it was not lived in by the Walpole family until the middle of the 19th century when it was extended by the eccentric 4th Earl of Orford. Mannington clearly appealed to the 4th Earl's antiquarian tastes. In the 1860s he added a substantial wing and further alterations were made by his nephew, the 5th Earl, in the 1890s. Some of the additions made by the 4th Earl are difficult to identify – which of the many gargoyles are original? Everyone notices the Latin inscriptions but perhaps, fortunately, not everyone can read them as they are all about the appalling qualities of women.

Mannington was let to tenants until 1969 when I moved in, working both on the restoration of the house and creating the present gardens. There was little historical detail available about the gardens which gave me plenty of scope to exercise my imagination and to introduce my own designs. Around the Hall are colour-themed borders, a scented garden laid out in the pattern of the plasterwork Dining Room ceiling and rose beds of rectangular shapes to echo the battlements. The old Kitchen Garden was laid out in 1980 as a 'Heritage Rose Garden' where small gardens, each designed to reflect a particular historical period, are planted with the appropriate roses.

In order to conserve the special landscapes at Mannington, we established the Countryside Management Plan in 1986, employing full time conservation staff. An Arboretum devoted to native species has been planted and the broadleaved and evergreen trees are now maturing well in groups relating to their usual habitat. There are woodland walks, a bamboo grove and, near the lake, members of the family planted trees for the Millennium. The Estate includes various areas of ancient woodland but the oldest and most exciting is the delightfully named 'Mossymere'. Here, as well as trees, are flowers including bluebells and orchids and abundant wildlife.

Whilst Wolterton houses the Estate offices, Mannington remains our family home. Working in one beautiful house and living in another makes the effort involved worthwhile.

Mellerstain

Gordon, Berwickshire

Whiteside House and the surrounding Mellerstain lands were confiscated in 1684 on the execution for high treason of Robert Baillie, a staunch supporter of the Covenanter movement. His impoverished son, George, fled to Holland with Sir Patrick Hume, later the Earl of Marchmont.

Returning in 1688 with the Prince of Orange, who was to become William III of England, the two families had their estates restored and were auspiciously linked in the marriage of George Baillie to Grisell Hume, Sir Patrick's beautiful and accomplished daughter. Her fabled heroism in childhood, delivering messages to the ill-fated Robert Baillie imprisoned in the Edinburgh Tolbooth, and in sustaining her father in hiding at Polwarth, as well as her classic 'Household Book', distinguish her as the most famous character in the history of Mellerstain. In 1725 she and George set about building the house at Mellerstain, with the architect William Adam, in the Dutch style – but only the two wings were completed and the central block that would join them never saw the light of day.

The younger son of their daughter Rachel, who married Charles, Lord Binning, heir to the Earl of Haddington, inherited Mellerstain in 1759. He assumed the Baillie name and, with Robert Adam, William's son, finally completed the magnificent classical centrepiece, with the splendid interiors and furniture he had grown to admire on the Grand Tour. It was not until 1858, when another George Baillie succeeded his second cousin as 10th Earl of Haddington, that the fortunes of Tyninghame, the Haddington seat in East Lothian, and Mellerstain were joined.

The house remained unchanged but his grandson, Lord Binning, who died during the First World War, commissioned Sir Reginald Blomfield in 1909 to transform the park on the south front of the house into garden terraces above the Lake. My father, the 12th Earl, devoted to his heritage, replaced many of the ancient woodlands felled to service the War effort, and planted thousands of new trees which now shape the landscape at Tyninghame and Mellerstain. He first opened Mellerstain to the public in 1952, a pioneer in the stately homes business. With my family, I strive to continue the work in this unspoilt and glorious spot.

Muncaster Castle

Ravenglass, Cumbria

Phyllida Gordon-Duff-Pennington

Muncaster has been the home of my family, the Penningtons, since at least 1208 when the lands were granted to Alan de Penitone. In about 1300, to repel Scottish raiders, the present pele tower was built over the remains of a Roman fort. In the eight centuries that followed, the Castle has never been sold and three generations of Penningtons currently live here.

There is the legend of the 'Luck of Muncaster', an enamelled glass bowl given to the family by the fugitive King Henry VI following his defeat at the Battle of Hexham in 1464, when he was sheltered and hidden at Muncaster by Sir John de Pennington. On his departure the King, to show his gratitude to the family, left his drinking bowl saying "As *long as this cup remains unriven Penningtons from Muncaster never shall be driven*". It is safe inside the Castle, and the family remain.

As the threat of border raids subsided, successive generations added to and altered the Castle to accommodate current tastes. The last major additions and alterations were carried out by the 4th Lord Muncaster who, in 1860-63, engaged the fashionable architect of the day, Salvin, to rebuild the house. This gave the Castle its Victorian air, while retaining echoes of its medieval past. Muncaster houses a fine collection of family portraits, silver, tapestries, oriental carpets and porcelain. The most striking portrait is not of a family member but of Thomas Skelton, manager and 'Fool' of Muncaster, who has given the English language the word 'tomfoolery'.

The Castle commands superb views of the surrounding Lakeland fells, being described by Ruskin as "*The Gateway to Paradise*". It sits in over 77 acres of wild woodland gardens, with extensive and important collections of acid-loving plants, especially rhododendrons, which thrive in the mild climate influenced by the proximity of the Gulf Stream. Muncaster has one of the longest continuous plant-hunting traditions of any UK garden, with plants contributed by Sir Joseph Hooker right up to 21st century introductions.

The World Owl Trust, a charity which since 1972 has pioneered conservation of owls and their environment worldwide, has its headquarters at Muncaster and operates the very popular World Owl Centre.

Millennium Commission and English Heritage grants at the end of the 20th century have ensured improved facilities for the Castle's many visitors for decades to come. My family live in the Castle and are intimately involved with all aspects of welcoming visitors to the revitalised Muncaster.

Phyllida Gordon Duff Pennington

Phyllida Gordon-Duff-Pennington

Newby Hall

Ripon, North Yorkshire

My family have lived at Newby Hall since 1748 when it was bought for my ancestor, William Weddell. The main block of the house was built in the 1690s by Sir Christopher Wren's number two, John Etty, for the then owner, Sir Edward Blackett. Celia Fiennes, visiting Newby on her tour of the north in 1697, recorded in her diary, 'This was the finest house I saw in Yorkshire'. In the 1760s Weddell, a prominent member of dilettanti society, made the Grand Tour; amongst the treasures he acquired were magnificent classical sculptures and a superb set of Gobelin tapestries. To house this very fine collection, Weddell commissioned the architect Robert Adam to create the splendid domed Sculpture Gallery and Tapestry Room that we see today. Indeed, the entire contents of the Tapestry Room are still in their original condition, which makes the room unique. Newby also has many fine pieces of Chippendale furniture, porcelain and paintings.

Weddell died in 1792 without children and Newby passed to his cousin, Thomas Philip Robinson, the 3rd Lord Grantham. At the beginning of the 19th century Grantham, a keen amateur architect and later president of the RIBA, built the Regency Dining Room; it is in marked contrast to Adam's fine mouldings and the graceful elegance of the rest of the house – an elegance restored in recent years by my mother who painstakingly researched Adam's original colour scheme. Later additions came in the form of a Victorian Wing housing the Billiards Room, added by Lord Grantham's grandson, Robert de Grey Vyner.

Some 25 acres of extensive gardens, laid out in the 1920s by my grandfather and since developed and enhanced by my father, are full of rare and beautiful plants. The main axis of the garden runs from the south front of the House right down to the River Ure and comprises the famous double Herbaceous Borders flanked by bold hedges of yew. Off this central walk are numerous formal compartmented gardens such as the Autumn Garden and species Rose Garden, a Victorian Rock Garden, a Water Garden and a Tropical Garden, each filled with plants to be at their best for the different seasons of the year – truly a 'Garden for all Seasons'. Newby also holds the National Collection of the genus *Cornus* (Dogwoods).

Richard Compton

Norton Conyers

Ripon, North Yorkshire

The name Norton Conyers is a combination of the Anglo-Saxon place name Norton (North Village), under which the property appears in Domesday Book, and the family name of its subsequent Norman owners. In the late 14th century the house passed to the Nortons, a wealthy and important family who lost all their lands through participating in the Rising of the North in 1569. Norton Conyers then passed to the Musgrave family and in 1624, to the Grahams who, except for a brief interval in the 19th century, have owned it ever since. Thus, the interior of the house, with its accumulated pictures and furniture, reflects almost 380 years of occupation by the same family.

Norton Conyers' most dramatic event was the sudden death of the 4th baronet (the present owner's great, great, great, great, grandfather) in 1755. He drank poisoned tea intended for his housekeeper, whose violent temper had made her very unpopular with the other servants. (That she was her employer's mistress and had given him three children cannot have made the situation any easier.) Despite an investigation, the culprit was never identified.

Norton Conyers is best known for its connection with Charlotte Brontë who paid a visit in 1839. She was much impressed by the legend of 'Mad Mary' who, in the previous century, had been confined to a remote attic room in the house. When Charlotte came to write *Jane Eyre*, she used the story as the basis for the mad Mrs Rochester and Norton Conyers certainly contributed some details to the model on which Thornfield Hall was based.

The architectural history of the House is extremely complicated. Recent research suggests that the larger part of the present building dates from the late 14th or early 15th centuries, with additions in the 16th, 17th, 18th and 19th centuries. Both inside and out, the house is a mixture of periods and styles. Almost every successive generation has left its mark on the exterior, the interior, or the grounds.

The nearby walled garden was probably constructed in the mid-18th century. Its main feature, an orangery with adjoining greenhouses, is approached up a slight slope between herbaceous borders flanked by tall yew hedges. It is in full cultivation. We hope it will long remain so.

James B. Graham

Sir James Graham Bt

Pashley Manor Gardens

Ticehurst, East Sussex

James Sellick

A grant of lands of some 700 acres was given by Henry III to Sir Edmund de Passele in 1262 and he built the original moated house here soon after. The de Passele family held the estate until 1453 when it was sold to Sir Geoffrey Boleyn, great grandfather of Anne Boleyn; it is most probable that Anne, second wife of Henry VIII, would have stayed here during her childhood.

At this time, the estate was mainly used for sporting purposes. Sir Thomas May, a successful Iron Master, purchased the property in 1540 and it was he who built the present manor. The house is unusual in having both a Tudor and an early Georgian façade, added in 1720. The Mays, a major Sussex family, owned the house for nearly 400 years. Thereafter, Pashley was unoccupied from 1922–1945 (except for brief periods by troops and evacuees) and has only in the last 20 years been restored to its present condition.

The earliest record of cultivation at Pashley is a garden wall built during the 15th century, and there are great oaks dating from the 15th and 16th centuries. However, much of the structure of the garden was formed in the mid-19th century, with the planting of fine specimen conifers. From this era also dates a beautiful period greenhouse, containing many interesting plants.

We first opened the Gardens to the public in 1992, having brought them to their present condition with the assistance of eminent landscape architect, Anthony du Gard Pasley. Within the old walled garden, a rose garden now flourishes, fine beds sweep across the South Front, enclosing the wide lawn sloping down to the moat where an ornamental bridge leads to the Island with its classical temple. Verdant walks, glades and a chain of large ponds provide many exceptional views of the house, fountains and sculptures, Brightling Beacon and the surrounding countryside.

From April to September each year we have an exciting programme of events at Pashley including the Tulip Festival in early May, our Spring and Summer Plant Fairs, the Summer Flower Festival, Sussex Craft Show in August, a Botanical Art Exhibition, and the Sculpture Exhibition which runs throughout the season.

James Sellick

James Sellick

Pencarrow

Bodmin, Cornwall

Pencarrow has been lived in by the Molesworths and their descendants, the Molesworth-St Aubyns, since the 16th century. The house has changed a great deal over the centuries, with its Palladian front and rococo plasterwork, the overall effect being Georgian.

An interesting, radical politician and an ardent and tireless reformer, Sir William Molesworth 8th Baronet, lived here during the 1830s. He not only designed the beautiful sunken Italian Garden but also created a great granite rockery made of huge boulders. He was responsible for constructing a drive, a mile long, through an Iron Age hilltop fort, planting up the American Garden with trees and shrubs from the Americas and finally making a lake and ice house. Due to Sir William's work and to my husband carefully replacing dead trees, the garden is now listed II*.

In the 1960s, my husband took over the running of the 2,500 acre estate, a large proportion being non-profitable woodlands. The house had stood empty for 18 years and was sulking and damp and the garden very overgrown – a daunting but rewarding task to see something so depressed come alive again. In 1975, the house was opened to the public for the first time, showing only a few rooms, one day a week. Now we show fourteen rooms and are open five days, sometimes seven in the spring, when the gardens are at their best.

We hope there is something for everyone at Pencarrow. For art lovers there is a superb collection of paintings by Arthur Devis, Samuel Scott, Richard Wilson, Henry Raeburn, Sir Joshua Reynolds and other well known artists set among outstanding collections of porcelain and furniture, including the piano used by Sir Arthur Sullivan when he stayed here in 1882 and composed much of the music for 'Iolanthe'.

It is so encouraging to be told by visitors how much they enjoyed their guided tour and that their dogs were delighted to be off the lead. We encourage children to roll down the banks in the Italian Garden as our grandchildren do, and try to make the tour of the house interesting for them. Many tell us in later years how, as unwilling visitors, they were dragged by their parents away from the nearby beaches at Rock and Polzeath, only to discover that visiting an historic house could also be fun.

Iona Molesworth-St Aubyn

Powderham Castle

Exeter, Devon

Many of today's surviving estates were founded on fortunes made in the Industrial Revolution. Powderham is one of the minority of survivors from an earlier era of Royal patronage, warfare and, no doubt, some good old fashioned pillaging in the 13th and 14th centuries. Nor did such activities necessarily cease altogether thereafter. In the late 18th century the Master of the Yacht was by far the most highly paid employee and no doubt augmented the estate's income with some lucrative privateering.

In the reign of Edward I, the Manor of Powderham was held by John de Powderham, but when male heirs were not forthcoming, it passed to the Bohuns, Earls of Hereford and Essex. The manor was part of Lady Margaret de Bohun's dowry when she married Hugh Courtenay, 2nd Earl of Devon in 1325 and on her death, she bequeathed it to her sixth son, Sir Philip Courtenay, my direct ancestor.

The origin of the name Powderham is believed to be 'Poulderham', a hamlet on a tidal marsh. It is not known for certain whether there was an earlier building on the castle site, but as it commanded both the River Exe and River Kenn, it is likely that there was a tower to guard against invasion. The present building was begun by Sir Philip Courtenay in about 1391 and extended during the following century. It was severely damaged in the Civil War and throughout the 18th century, much work was done internally and externally, making it harder to visualise the medieval Castle. Lastly came the alterations carried out by William, 10th Earl of Devon who, with the help of an Exeter architect, Charles Fowler, added the Victorian courtyard.

The grounds of the Castle have much to occupy visitors of all ages. As well as walks and the Woodland Garden, there is a terraced Rose Garden overlooking an ancient deer park, home to a large herd of fallow deer. The Rose Garden is home to Timothy the Tortoise who, at over 160 years old, is the world's most senior pet.

The Castle has always been, and still remains, a family home to which successive generations of my family have made additions and alterations to suit the fashion and needs of their time. Many feel this adds greatly to its interest and charm. It is one of the very few great houses in England to have remained in the family who built it for more than 600 years.

The Earl of Devon

Prideaux Place

Padstow, Cornwall

In her wonderfully eclectic book on unwrecked England, Candida Lycett Green describes Prideaux Place as *"about as unwrecked as you can get"* and its estate as (standing in) *"miles of beautiful coast unwrecked, unadulterated and not owned by the National Trust"*. Some houses have architects while others just seem to have settled into the land they so anciently occupy and nowhere could this be truer than Prideaux Place, built in 1588 by its eponymous family who trace their lineage even further back through 1,000 years of Cornish history. Fourteen generations of Prideaux have stamped their own proud individuality on this sprawling 80-room mansion, which stands as a robust rebuke to the mediocrity of the planning officer and all his works. Here, in short, is a house and family organically growing together according to their own needs and whims.

The Elizabethan front of Prideaux Place is built in the shape of an E in honour of the reign that begat it, but pass through its stout front door and you walk through a succession of rooms from different ages that were born as they were needed – the panelled Elizabethan dining room, the oval Strawberry Hill drawing room, the Restoration Grenville Room with its gilded Grinling Gibbons carvings, the fan-vaulted Gothick library – all these and more culminate in the magnificence of the first floor Great Chamber with its 16th century plaster ceiling depicting some of the racier aspects of the Old Testament.

If the house is individual this is surely reflected in the rugged independence of its family who backed the wrong side in both the Civil War and Monmouth's rebellion and who earlier, in a well documented incident, shot and wounded a Crown Commissioner sent to Padstow to investigate a spot of freelance privateering in 1591.

Today Prideaux Place goes on fulfilling its original purpose as headquarters to a family, an estate and a community. Do not look here for Palladio, William Kent or even Le Corbusier, for you will find only a deeply original and indigenous England where an ancient family quietly continues.

Peter Prideaux-Brune

Raby Castle

Darlington, Co. Durham

The magnificent Raby Castle, in the beautiful North Pennines, has been home to my family since 1626, when it was purchased by my ancestor, Sir Henry Vane the Elder, the eminent statesman and politician.

The Castle was built mainly in the 14th century by the Nevill family on a site of an earlier manor house. The Nevills continued to live at Raby until 1569 when, after the failure of the Rising of the North, the Castle and its land were forfeited to the Crown.

During the Civil War Raby was besieged by the Royalists on five occasions. Fortunately the Castle suffered little damage and it was not until the 18th century that the first major alterations were made to the medieval structure. Daniel Garrett and James Paine were employed by Henry, 2nd Earl of Darlington, followed by John Carr who carried out extensive work.

The impressive Entrance Hall was created into its present dramatic form by John Carr for the 2nd Earl, to celebrate the coming of age of his heir in 1787. The roof was raised to enable carriages to pass through the Hall and the result is a stunning interior in the Gothic Revival style. By the end of the 18th century, not only the Castle but also its setting were considerably altered: the Moat was drained, the Park landscaped, the High and Low Ponds excavated, the Garden laid out and the Stables and ancillary buildings constructed.

The Octagon Drawing Room is by far the grandest room at Raby, being designed solely to impress. Created for the 2nd Duke of Cleveland in 1848 in the French style by the Scottish architect William Burn, it is a masterpiece. Now, following a major restoration programme which commenced in 1993, the room has re-emerged as one of the most striking interiors of a decade that loved rich lavish decoration, with its ornate gilt ceiling and magnificent silk damask wall coverings.

Raby's treasures include an important collection of Meissen porcelain, fine furniture and artworks, including paintings by Munnings, De Hooch, Reynolds, Van Dyck, Batoni, Teniers, Amigoni, Vernet and De Vos.

Today we welcome thousands of visitors each year at Raby. There is a 200 acre Deer Park with two lakes and a beautiful walled garden. The 18th century stable block contains a horse-drawn carriage collection, including the State Coach which was last used by my family for the Coronation of Edward VII in 1902.

Barnard

Rockingham Castle

Northamptonshire

Rockingham Castle's long royal history, and my family's 450 year association with it, has given the Castle a special, almost magical, quality.

In 1066 William the Conqueror recognised the importance of the site at Rockingham, on the brink of the Welland Valley escarpment, building the Castle as an administrative centre and a base for hunting in the surrounding forest. The Castle still has its original Norman plan – a massive wall with two square towers, surrounding an outer bailey which contained the Great Hall, Chapel and living quarters for up to 3,000 people.

Throughout the 12th century, Rockingham was visited regularly by successive kings, in particular King John who left behind his treasure chest which remains here today, still awaiting collection. During the reign of Edward I, the primitive Norman castle was modernised – windows and a fireplace were created in the Great Hall and a bedroom installed in the eaves for his beloved Queen, Eleanor of Castile.

In 1544 my ancestor, Edward Watson, through his family connections at Court, secured a lease on the Castle and Park of Rockingham. The work of converting the derelict medieval castle into a comfortable Tudor residence took 30 years to complete. Edward's grandson, Sir Lewis Watson, bought the castle outright in 1619. Unfortunately, during the Civil War, the Castle fell to the Parliamentary forces and although the property was eventually returned to Sir Lewis, it had suffered considerable damage. Sir Lewis and his son restored the Castle over many years.

Few changes were made during the 18th century and it was not until 1836, when Richard Watson inherited, that a major modernisation programme was embarked upon, employing the architect Anthony Salvin. A flag tower was added to the Gallery wing which today houses a collection of weapons and other artefacts. Richard's son, George, died in 1899 without producing an heir and the Castle passed to his brother, the Reverend Wentworth Watson who made some important alterations to the interior. He also died childless in 1925 and the Castle was inherited by his great nephew, Sir Michael Culme Seymour. He and his wife, Lady Faith Montagu, did much to modernise the Castle and the village. A portrait of Sir Michael, my great uncle, hangs in the Panel Room watching over us today. In order to avoid crippling death duties, he handed over the Castle in 1971 to his nephew, my father, who in turn passed it on to me in 1999.

James Saunders Watson

Rode Hall

Scholar Green, Cheshire

Roger Wilbraham of Townsend House, Nantwich, purchased Rode for his younger son, Randle, in 1669 for £2,600. The main part of the house that exists today was built in 1752 and significantly remodelled some 50 years later: the bows were added, the windows lowered and stucco was applied to the whole building. It was not until 1927 that the stucco was removed from the house and the main entrance redesigned by Darcy Braddell.

The interior of the house was changed significantly in the early part of the 19th century and following the death of the architect, John Hope, who had been working at Rode, Lewis Wyatt completed the work to the interior. The main staircase hall, however, is the one part of the house that is still in its original state.

Following the alterations in 1812, Gillow of Lancaster supplied the furniture for the principal rooms on the ground floor and the dining room in particular contains fine examples of Gillow's work. There is an excellent collection of portraits in the house from both the Wilbraham and the Baker families. Sir George Baker, the direct descendant of Dr Baker, physician to George III, married Katharine Wilbraham who was to inherit Rode on the death of her father in 1900. The house also contains an important collection of English porcelain, including a fine Derby dessert service that was commissioned by Mary Bootle in 1787.

It was Mary Bootle, also, who commissioned Humphry Repton to produce a 'Red Book' for Rode in 1790. Although Repton was not invited to carry out his plans, the work was undertaken by John Webb some 10 years later and reflected many of the ideas suggested by Repton. Webb was responsible also for the laying out of the terraced rock garden, which has the only surviving grotto in Cheshire. This part of the garden is splendid in May and early June when the rhododendrons and azaleas are at their best.

The formal garden was designed by Nesfield in 1860 and remains sympathetic to his original plans, and there is a large walled kitchen garden dating back to the mid-18th century in which many varieties of fruit and vegetables are grown.

Rode and the surrounding estate remain one of the totally unspoilt parts of Cheshire, despite being within a short distance of the Potteries. It is very much a family home and, with a son and a grandson to follow my stewardship, it promises to continue to be a much treasured home for many years to come.

R Baker Wilbraham

Sand

Sidmouth, Devon

Amongst the documents we have is the earliest surviving deed of a house at Sand. This dates from the middle of the 13th century showing the land was granted by the Dean and Chapter of Exeter to William de Saunde and his son Deodatus. The property then passed to John Hitteway de Sande and was sold to the Tremayle family, who held it for over a century. The medieval hall house, the original roof structure of which survives, is likely to have been built by the Tremayles in early 1400, as was a small chapel that was burnt down in 1830.

By the early 1500s, a second house had been built close to the hall house and the whole estate was purchased in 1560 by Henry Huyshe of Rodhuish in Somerset. Henry left Sand to his sons who sold it to their father's first cousin James Huyshe. James not only succeeded in making a fortune in London but also fathered 28 children. This sale in 1584 was the last time that the land at Sand was sold. On James' death, his eldest son Rowland enlarged the newer house and created the Elizabethan building you see today – the same house in which we, his descendants, still live. The adjacent medieval hall house remained, and eventually became a barn.

In 1610 Rowland built a delightful thatched summer house, experimenting with Palladian pillars, and many of his documents have been passed down including a diary, house inventory and his handwritten translation of Cicero's *de Senectute*. His son, James, was actively engaged on the Royalist side in the Civil War, though his two elder daughters married captains in the Parliamentary army. The house was let as a farmhouse for almost 250 years but has remained in our family possession. In 1910 my uncle, a second Rowland Huyshe, updated the building and restored a wing which had been destroyed by fire.

Nestling in a tranquil valley, the house and garden have evolved over the centuries, reflecting Devon's fortunes and the family's changing requirements. Sand is very much our home. None of it is mothballed, and none of it a museum. It stands, in the 21st century, rooted in its history but still moving onwards; we have three generations involved in public openings, and it is still lived in and loved.

P. V. Huyshe.

Scone Palace

Perth, Perthshire

Our Papal Bull of 1208 elevates Scone from Monastery to Abbey, thus continuing Scone's already ancient and unique history. While the Romans tramped through the park, the Picts made awkward bedfellows, as Scone was then their capital. The Moot Hill of Scone was scene to the coronation of no less than 48 Kings of Scots, amongst whom were MacBeth and Robert the Bruce (1306), the last being Charles II, his being the only Presbyterian crowning ever held.

Christianity had been accepted here by the Pictish King Nectan in about 900, on behalf of an unwilling populace. All ceremony centred on The Stone of Scone from 800 to 1296, when Edward of England, Hammer of the Scots, fought his way here to remove the Regalia of Scotland and impose his own law court. The Palace of Scone, hard by the Abbey, was an on-off residence for the then necessarily itinerant monarchs.

Scone Palace, today, is a large castellated sandstone house whose most recent major modernisation had been completed by 1804 by Atkinson, but encapsulated many earlier palaces. In rebuilt walls can be found 13th century pillars and carved stones, and 12th century human burials have surprised plumbers working on drains by the front door, as has the Roman glass in the asparagus! Within the lofty but restrained Gothic exterior, is to be seen 400 years of our family's acquisitiveness since arriving at Scone.

The Palace, having housed these monarchs, became the property of the Earl of Gowrie. When that family was accused of attempting to murder James VI and I, the palace and lands were awarded to Sir David Murray, who became Lord Stormont. Descendants of this family became Earls of Mansfield in the mid 18th century, with the startlingly brilliant 1st Earl being Lord Chief Justice and Lord Chancellor for 32 years concurrently. With his equally brilliant nephew, who became 2nd Earl, they would go on shopping sprees to Paris where his nephew, Viscount Stormont, was Ambassador. The results of their shopaholic tendencies are to be seen in the sumptuous collections on view at Scone — of porcelain, furniture, ivories, pictures and so on.

The pleasure grounds at Scone are made up of rolling lawns, ancient stones, a 13th century village cross, a Wild Garden, Butterfly Garden and Scented Garden, magnificent trees and the Pinetum, planted in 1829, containing giant sequoias. The Murray Star Maze is also very popular. These, together with many different events held throughout the year, have made Scone Palace a place of continual "happenings".

Mansfield

Somerleyton Hall

Lowestoft, Suffolk

There has been a House on the site at Somerleyton since the 13th century. The present Hall was created between 1844 and 1851 by the great Victorian entrepreneur, Sir Morton Peto, by enlarging and embellishing an earlier Jacobean Mansion House, a transformation which epitomised that era of self-confident expansion.

The house we see today is unmistakably an early Victorian invention, built without regard for expense; stone was imported from Caen, Italianate and French Renaissance effects were used with abandon and paintings specially commissioned. In 1861 however, Sir Morton, having suffered a dramatic downturn in his fortunes, was forced to put the house and its contents on the market and in 1863 it was bought, lock, stock and barrel, by Sir Francis Crossley, another entrepreneur who had made a fortune from the manufacture of carpets in Halifax, Yorkshire. He was my great grandfather. Sir Francis' son, Sir Savile, was created Baron Somerleyton in 1916.

The house has lavish Anglo-Italian style architectural features. Apart from the demolition of the Winter Garden in 1914, the only major change to the house since 1863 was during my grandfather's time in the 1920s, when he divided Peto's enormous Banqueting Hall, creating the Library with bedrooms above.

The gardens and grounds at Somerleyton have been popular with visitors since the 19th century and as early as 1863, on Thursday afternoons (early closing day in Lowestoft), horse-drawn coaches would bring people to visit. In 1981 a new avenue of limes, *Tilia cordata*, was planted and the ever popular yew hedge Maze was substantially cut back in the 1970s to encourage fresh new growth.

I inherited Somerleyton in 1959 and together with my wife, Belinda, and our five children, we are the fourth generation of Crossleys to live in the Hall. We feel we have achieved a lot up to the present day. Having come through a deep depression in the 1950s, when many historic houses were demolished, things started to look up in the 1960s when repair grants became available. Since 1964 we have gradually improved the building by replacing the roof and chimneys and the original, badly eroded soft Caen stone used by Peto, with harder Pine and Chipsham stones. With the help of English Heritage, the main repairs and restoration work are now nearly complete. Somerleyton Hall is our family home where children and grandchildren are very much in evidence to this day.

Somerleyton

Squerryes Court

Westerham, Kent

Squerryes Court, set in a natural bowl overlooking the lake with the Surrey hills in the background, is built of mellow brick with a steep-pitched slate roof and timber cornice in the classic style. Although altered over the years it has retained most of the original features. A substantial timbered hall house had stood on the site before the present house was built by Sir Nicholas Crisp, a London merchant, in 1682. Following Sir Nicholas' death six years later, it was acquired by the 1st Earl of Jersey who, in 1700 added three pavilions and created the formal gardens. The influence of Hampton Court on the 1st Earl, following his time spent there as Lord Chamberlain and Master of the Horse to William III, is plain to see in the 1719 Badeslade print of the house and gardens.

In 1732, John Warde, son of Sir John Warde (a Lord Mayor of London, MP and Governor of the Bank of England) bought the house from his friend, the 3rd Earl of Jersey. Squerryes has been home to the Warde family ever since. Squire John Warde (1755 – 1839) became renowned in the sporting world as the father of foxhunting, whilst his uncle, two brothers and two nephews were distinguished generals. Another nephew who inherited Squerryes was an admiral who had fought under Nelson as a young officer.

The Wardes, an old landed family from Yorkshire who became wealthy merchants, filled the house with a fine collection of furniture, tapestries, porcelain and pictures which was added to over the years and most of which remains in the house today. Lord Jersey's pavilions were demolished c1830 and wings containing kitchens, domestic services and the servants' quarters were added to the main house, only to be demolished in 1948 and the house restored to its original shape.

In the mid-18th century, the gardens were landscaped in the style of Brown and Repton, sweeping away the walls, basin and other formal features. A wild garden with rhododendrons and azaleas was planted during the 19th century and a rockery also established. The house was then let until after the Second World War and much of the garden became neglected and overgrown. The great storm of 1987, which felled 150 trees, provided the opportunity for us to begin an ambitious programme of restoration of the gardens, with the help of Tom Wright. This started with the planting of formal parterres, hedges, lime trees and borders, using the 1719 plan of the formal garden for inspiration and themes, and continues today.

John St A. Warde

Stanford Hall

Lutterworth, Leicestershire

This exquisite William and Mary house, set in its own park on the River Avon, was built in the 1690s for Sir Roger Cave to the designs of William Smith of Warwick. The Caves, my direct ancestors, have farmed the land at Stanford since 1430, living previously on the Northamptonshire side of the river. In the Library is the detailed estimate from Smith for pulling down the old house and building the present for a sum of £2,137.10s.7d. In all, over a period of some 50 years, three members of the Cave family employed three members of the Smith family to build and embellish their house and stables – the result is unusually cohesive and pure. It is perhaps fortunate that the only subsequent (1880s) addition to the buildings got dry rot in the 1920s and had to be pulled down!

The house contains a collection of fine pictures and furniture, mainly 18th century, some earlier. The books in the Library, numbering over 5000, were chosen and read by successive members of the family, just as the costumes in the Old Dining Room were worn by them. The most interesting pictures are the 'Stuart Collection' of Royal Stuart portraits purchased in Rome in 1842 by Sarah, 3rd Baroness Braye, from the estate of the Cardinal Duke of York, younger brother of Prince Charles Edward. The finest of these shows the three eldest children of Charles I – the future Charles II, Mary, the future mother of King William of Orange, and the future James II. This dynastically important picture belonged to James II and went with him into exile. More Stuart pictures, including the last major portrait of Prince Charles Edward, hang in the lovely pink and gold Ballroom. The Ballroom is still lit using a 110 volt supply, resulting from the 6th Lord Braye's ingenious electrical enterprises in the 1890s which involved diverting the River Avon, installing a turbine, and deploying a team of ferrets!

I am the third woman in my family to inherit both the place and the peerage through direct descent, which has made names rather confusing. I succeeded my father, the 7th Lord Braye, on his death in 1985. Stanford has been my home since 1958 and I have lived there since 1981 with my husband, Colonel Edward Aubrey-Fletcher, who has shared my great enthusiasm for this beautiful house. Now – in early 2003 – I am handing on Stanford to another generation of my family, to my cousin, Nicholas Fothergill and his wife Lucy. We hope that they will enjoy living at Stanford as much as we have done.

Penelope Braye

Stanway House & Water Garden

Cheltenham, Gloucestershire

Stanway has about it a timelessness, an almost magical feeling of having avoided the less pleasant aspects of the modern age, which is apparent even to the most casual visitor. This is partly because of the protection of the Cotswold escarpment, which rises dramatically for 700' behind the village, partly from continuity of ownership and partly because of the deep love its beauty has inspired in owners and inhabitants alike over the centuries.

The extraordinary variety of the escarpment, with its intimate wooded valleys and streams linking wold to vale, the charm of the parkland with its ancient oaks and chestnuts, coppices and stone walls and the traditional, vernacular architecture of almost all the buildings, provide a perfect setting for the Jacobethan manor house in the hamlet of Church Stanway.

The Tracy family had the unique distinction of having owned land in Gloucestershire before the Norman Conquest, and of descent from Charlemagne. In an age when hereditary right counted, they enjoyed a prestige and self-confidence in the county which gave them little ambition to excel outside it – they were Justices, High Sheriffs and MPs – and may have contributed to the sureness of their aesthetic and social touch at Stanway.

Prestige and self-confidence notwithstanding, Sir William Tracy (d 1530) was posthumously burnt at the stake for expressing Lutheran opinions in his will, which encouraged his younger son, Richard Tracy MP, to dabble in religious politics and, with Thomas Cromwell's help, to acquire a lease of Stanway from the soon-to-be-dissolved Abbey of Tewkesbury in 1533. His descendants refenestrated and gabled the west front and added the jewel-like gatehouse and the serene south front c 1630.

The family backed the King in the Civil War, and had to pay a colossal fine of £1,600 to Parliamentary sequestrators to avoid losing the estate. John Tracy (1680-1735) and his wife found time, in between rearing 15 children, to engage a landscape architect of genius – probably Charles Bridgeman whose work at Rousham they admired – to create one of the finest water gardens in England, which has been partially restored and, with the addition of a magnificent single-jet fountain, should be completed by 2005.

In 1771 the last Tracy heiress married Francis Charteris, son of the 7th Earl of Wemyss from East Lothian, and it is therefore the Earls of Wemyss who have since 1817 cherished the very special architectural, social and landscape entity created by the Tracys.

The Lord Neidpath

Stobhall

Guildtown, Perthshire

Stobhall is the original Drummond property, coming into the family in the mid 14th century by marriage to the heiress of the Monfichet family. It has been in different branches of the family ever since. Its position and natural charm are the most striking things about Stobhall. A romantic, if somewhat impractical house, it consists of several separate buildings. Guests often have to go outside, across the courtyard, to get to their bedrooms – very sobering after dinner in the depths of winter.

The earliest building is the Chapel from the 14th century and the small castle attached to it is late 16th century. In the Chapel, the painted ceiling from the 1640s is naïve and wonderful. It displays the mounted monarchs of Europe including Charles 1 and a splendid King of Mauretania on an elephant.

Before the First World War our own seat at Strathallan had been sold. When my grandfather succeeded his father as Earl of Perth in 1951 he set out to restore the family fortune. In 1953 his friend and kinsman James, Earl of Ancaster, offered my grandparents the partly ruined Stobhall, then about to be given to the Ministry of Works. He thought them quite mad as the house was in terrible condition and threatening to collapse into the den below.

Restoring the buildings and garden at Stobhall became my grandparents' project for the next forty-five years. They had an enormous amount of fun, including building a library to complete the group of buildings, creating one of Scotland's most attractive small castles. I hope visitors agree that it was worth their efforts.

Stonor

Henley-on-Thames, Oxfordshire

My family has always lived here. A Stonor built the first house, and the estate passed from father to son in direct succession – except three times, twice when succession was to a younger brother, and once to a grandson – for 850 years. It is one of the very few houses in England to have remained in the same family from earliest records to the present day.

House building, development and improvements all coincided with times when the family have prospered – notably from the 12th - 16th centuries, and again from the mid-18th century. In between, they lived privately and little expansion or improvement was possible, since heavy recusancy fines had to be paid as a result of the family's adherence to their faith.

My parents began a period of prolonged and much-needed restoration after the Second World War. However, the house and park were put up for sale upon my father's death in 1976. Fortunately, I was able to save them. When my wife and I returned to Stonor in 1978, apart from most of the family portraits and the books in the Library (which I purchased later), the house was empty.

Fortunately my cousin, Francis Stonor, had, in 1968, bequeathed to me his distinguished collection of furniture, pictures, bronzes and rugs. Similarly, my aunts and family friends have kindly made available some beautiful family objects, tapestries, portraits and furniture. Thus encouraged, we have saved every family portrait and by other purchases, have completed the refurnishing of the house.

Under the expert direction of my wife, the many repairs and redecoration that my parents could not achieve have been largely completed.

My wife has also totally redesigned and replanted what was the large kitchen garden. The surrounding walls and summerhouse have been repaired, and the Coach House made sound.

There is a great deal to see at Stonor and we are pleased to be able to show our visitors so many good examples of continuity of my family's residence here.

Camoys.

Stratfield Saye

Basingstoke, Hampshire

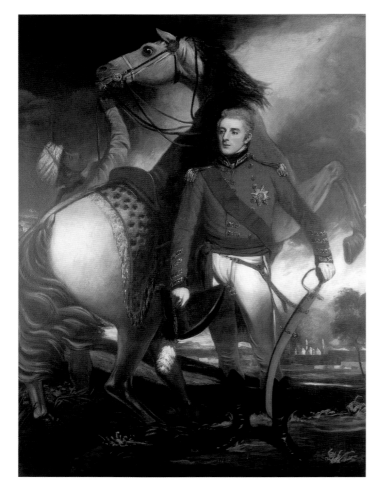

The main part of Stratfield Saye House was built in about 1635 for Sir William Pitt, Comptroller of the Household and a principal officer in the Exchequer in the reigns of Elizabeth I, James I and Charles I. It is on the site of an earlier manor house. The structure of the original Carolean house is practically unchanged, but the interior was extensively remodelled at various times, mostly by Sir William's great great grandson, George Pitt, 1st Baron Rivers, in the period 1740-1790. At this time the original red brick house was covered with stucco, which was painted white.

After the Battle of Waterloo, the Duke of Wellington was voted a sum of money by Parliament to purchase a suitable estate. He considered a number of houses including Bramshill and Uppark, but eventually chose Stratfield Saye for its proximity to London and Windsor. He was encouraged to demolish the house and build a vast Waterloo Palace to rival Blenheim Palace. A design competition was held and plans drawn up. The Duke gave up the idea after a few years due to lack of resources and eventually made a number of additions to the existing house. The conservatory and first and second floors to the outer wings were added in 1840. He also introduced central heating and water closets to numerous rooms, many of which remain in full working order.

The house is still occupied by the family and retains its character as the 1st Duke's country house. In the last few years considerable work has taken place to repair the roof, re-render the chimneys and to replace the cast iron gutters, lead valleys and downpipes. The South wing, which had been unoccupied since 1900, has been fully restored, including the installation for the first time of electric light. Central heating and running water have been reconnected to the original systems and the rooms refurnished wherever possible in accordance with the 1853 inventory.

Syon House

Brentford, Middlesex

Syon started life as a Bridgettine abbey built by Henry V in the early 15th century. Trumped-up charges of lascivious acts perpetrated by the principally female members of the order gave Henry VIII the excuse he needed to dissolve the Abbey in 1539 and confiscate the property, which remained in Royal hands until the early 17th century. When Henry died, his funeral cortège stopped at Syon for the night en route for Windsor and, as the assembly slept, his bloated body burst open and leaked through the coffin onto the floor. The following morning a dog was seen licking the King's blood from the ground, thereby fulfilling the curse of a Franciscan friar for the King's destruction of the Catholic Church.

The Lord Protector, the Duke of Somerset, is credited with starting the construction of the present house from the abbey buildings. After Somerset's execution, John Dudley, Duke of Northumberland (no relation to the Northumberland Percys) acquired Syon where his daughter-in-law, Lady Jane Grey, was offered the Crown. The later return of the Percy Earls of Northumberland to favour, after a period in the 'wilderness', brought Syon into my family's hands, first as tenants and then as owners – it was given to the 9th Earl of Northumberland by James I for services rendered. Despite the Earl's implication in the Gunpowder Plot (his cousin Thomas was a ring-leader) and his subsequent lengthy sojourn in the Tower, the house remained in Percy hands.

Syon, like Alnwick Castle, underwent a renaissance under the 1st Percy Duke and Duchess of Northumberland towards the end of the 18th century. The austere exterior of the house was in stark contrast to the jewel-box they created within. Robert Adam's work at Syon was one of his most significant and delightful achievements, and little has changed up to the present day.

'Capability' Brown's landscape, Charles Fowler's Great Conservatory, the beautiful gardens and lakes, and the River Thames flowing past the tidal water meadows, all make Syon a magical place. On bright summer days, with doors and windows thrown open to catch any passing breeze, it is a glorious place. On cold winter nights, however, its endless corridors, poor lighting, 'staring' portraits and creaky floor boards, can make the hairs stand up on the back of your neck! Maybe it is the spirits of the nuns, or the muted sobs of a headless Lady Jane Grey, that make those eerie noises at night.

Apart from the spooks, Syon houses a fabulous collection of paintings, sculptures and furniture, collected by my forebears from all over the world. A programme of restoration is now under way to ensure Syon's continued position as one of the great treasure houses of Britain.

Northumberland

Thorp Perrow Arboretum

Bedale, North Yorkshire

Set in the glorious North Yorkshire countryside just south of Bedale, Thorp Perrow Arboretum is a treasure trove of trees and shrubs established over 60 years ago by my father, Sir Leonard Ropner. The arboretum, covering 85 acres, was originally intended as a private personal collection but became, during the latter years of my father's life, rather neglected and overgrown so, on inheriting it in 1977, I began a major programme to restore it.

Today the arboretum contains one of the finest collections of trees and shrubs in Britain. With over 1,000 different species and varieties, it is a Mecca for plant lovers from all over the world. Indeed, amongst the rarities are several trees that are either the largest specimens in Britain or the only examples known to be in cultivation.

The arboretum holds four National Collections – *Tilia* (Lime), *Fraxinus* (Ash), *Juglans* (Walnut) and *Laburnum*. As well as a medieval Spring Wood, where some of the oak trees are believed to be over 400 years old, there is a Pinetum planted by Lady Augusta Milbank during the 1840s and 1850s.

Thorp Perrow has something to offer all year round. Spring bursts into colour with one of the largest displays of naturalised daffodils to be found in the north of England. This is followed with avenues of blossom, carpets of bluebells and bold drifts of wild flowers. Later in the year, the autumn foliage and colourful berries provide a spectacular display of dramatic and vivid colour.

We also have the 'Falcons of Thorp Perrow', a captive breeding and conservation centre, and one of the largest collections of birds of prey to be found in the north of England. Visitors have the opportunity to learn more about birds of prey and associated wildlife, with plenty of hands-on experience, including by children. Entertaining flying demonstrations with lively and informative commentary are held three times daily throughout the open season.

The arboretum provides a wonderful experience for visitors where there is freedom to enjoy the beauty of nature, children can safely explore, and the serious gardener or naturalist can revel in this treasure house of wonderful trees.

[signature]

Tissington Hall

Ashbourne, Derbyshire

Tissington Hall has been the home of my family, the FitzHerberts, for the past 500 years. Originally, the family came to England with William the Conqueror, settling in Derbyshire in 1125 when William FitzHerbert was granted the Manor of Norbury. The present Hall, built in 1609 by Francis FitzHerbert to replace the original moated manor house, has been embellished by each generation of the family and is a house of many extensions: a top floor was added c1700 and in 1780, the west aspect was remodelled by the well-known Derby architect, Joseph Pickford. The major extension of the Library and Billiard Room wing was completed in 1902 by the architect, Arnold Mitchell, for the 5th Baronet, Rev Sir Richard FitzHerbert.

Many of the rooms are magnificently panelled in oak, much dating from the 17th century and some rather more austere in style and unmistakably Victorian. The house contains fine collections of paintings, family portraits and furniture, with pieces by Chippendale in the Main Hall and Dining Room.

On inheriting the Hall and adjoining estate from my uncle in 1989, I spent a great deal of my early tenure on essential repairs to the property – re-roofing in 1991, re-wiring in 1992, and the re-plumbing project in 1998. I have, at the same time, endeavoured to make more effective use of our 'wasting assets' by converting redundant property into more useful enterprises: the Old Kitchen Garden is now a Plant Nursery; the Old Coach House has become a thriving Tearoom; the Old Joiners' Shop a successful Craft Shop and the Old Slaughterhouse is a Butchery for organic meat. Most recently the stables, which are earlier than the house, have been the subject of an award-winning conversion to accommodate a pre-prep school which is run by my wife.

Since June 1998 Tissington Hall has been open to the public for 28 days each summer, in addition to the various charity opening days that are publicised locally. I much prefer, however, to entertain groups and societies at any time throughout the year as they can benefit from having personal guided tours of the Hall and grounds, as well as gaining an intimate knowledge of the practicalities of living in such a house, home to our young family.

Torosay Castle

Isle of Mull, Argyll

Chris James

A fine example of Victorian country house building, Torosay was completed in 1858 by the architect David Bryce, leading exponent of the Scottish Baronial style. It combines an elegant and imposing exterior with bright and well-proportioned interiors and is laid out in a manner which takes full advantage of its splendidly scenic setting.

My family have lived here since 1865 when the Estate was purchased by my great, great, great uncle, Arbuthnot Guthrie. But we feel that its heyday would have been the decade after my great grandparents unexpectedly inherited in 1897. Guests included Winston Churchill, Nellie Melba, Frederick Selous and Admiral Charles Beresford, and it was at this time also that the statuary collection and the Italianate terraced gardens were added.

The Gardens are a special feature of Torosay; the contrast of the formal terraces and gazebos with the wild mountain and seascapes being most dramatic, enhanced by the superb collection of 18th century Italian statuary and a range of interesting plants which thrive in the mild – and moist – Hebridean climate. The newly restored water garden and several 'niche' gardens around the periphery provide a lovely setting for exploring and relaxing.

If Torosay's heyday was the start of the 20th century, then the last 20 years, during which the Castle has been managed as a business welcoming visitors, may also come to be seen as something of a renaissance. During this time it has been possible not only to restore buildings and care for the gardens, but also to consider the designed landscape. Most especially, the wooded knolls on the north, west and south of the Castle, which so enhance its setting and which were mostly given over to spruce trees some 50 years ago, are now being replanted more appropriately. Two of the most significant are being named after our children: Fenella's Wood is being planted solely with material from Chile as part of the International Conifer Conservation Programme while David's Wood will more closely follow the 19th century pattern of mixed planting.

The Castle contains some good, though relatively second order, paintings and the furnishings, while appropriate to the building, are from no particular period and are mostly undistinguished. This we see as a merit, allowing a more knockabout approach and enabling us to encourage our visitors to sit down, browse through family scrap books and treat the Castle as the home that it is.

Chris James

Chris James

Traquair House

Innerleithen, Peeblesshire

Catherine Maxwell Stuart

Traquair is said to be Scotland's oldest continually inhabited house and spans over 1,000 years of Scottish history.

Established as a hunting lodge for Scottish kings by the 12th century, it then became a defensive peel tower in the early 14th century when the calamitous wars of independence shattered the peace of the Border country. The house was occupied by English troops but returned to the Crown with the accession of Robert the Bruce in 1306. It remained in royal ownership until 1469 when King James III gifted the Castle to a favoured court musician, William Rogers, who then sold it, in 1478, for the paltry sum of 70 Scots Merks (£3.15s.10d), to the Earl of Buchan. Bestowed by the Earl on his son, James Stuart, later the 1st Laird of Traquair, the house has remained in Stuart ownership ever since.

In many ways it is remarkable that my family were able to retain the house and estate as they often found themselves on the wrong side both in politics and religion. In 1635 an earldom was granted to Sir John Stuart who attained the office of High Treasurer of Scotland, but this was to be short lived as the Earl fell out of favour with the King and reportedly ended his days begging in the streets of Edinburgh.

During the 18th century the Earls of Traquair were strong supporters of the Jacobite cause and played a part in both the 1715 and 1745 rebellions. It was then that the famous Bear Gates of Traquair were closed by the 5th Earl after wishing Bonnie Prince Charlie a safe journey and vowing they would never be opened until a Stuart King returned to the throne. They remain closed to this day.

The wings of the house were added in 1700 and in one of them a large domestic brewery was added, in common with many large country houses. Uniquely, however, although it remained unused in the 19th and early 20th centuries, it was not dismantled and was rediscovered by my father, 150 years later, who started to brew again in 1965. The dark, strong and delicious Traquair House Ale is still produced and sold throughout the world.

The house was first opened to the public in 1958 and we have gradually developed it as an attraction over the last 30 years. I was born here, and being brought up in a house open to the public was tremendous fun, and an endless source of jobs, working in the gift shop, washing up in the tea room and even cleaning out the brewery vessels with my father. Traquair is very much a piece of living history and we hope that all visitors here will experience its unique atmosphere that makes it such an extraordinary family home.

Catherine Maxwell Stuart

Warwick Castle

Warwick, Warwickshire

The origins of Warwick Castle can be traced back to Saxon fortification which Ethelfleda, daughter of Alfred the Great, used to defend against the invading Danes. The first castle to appear on the site, however, was a wooden motte-and-bailey constructed in 1068 at the command of William the Conqueror. Throughout the Middle Ages, under successive Earls of Warwick, the Castle was gradually rebuilt in stone and by the 14th century, it was a towering medieval fortress and the stronghold of the mighty Beauchamp family. Later, as the Castle declined in military importance, the main living quarters were converted into a residence of rich and sumptuous style, reflecting the wealth and status of its owners. Attacked in 1264, besieged in 1642 and damaged by fire in 1871, it has nevertheless gloriously survived the ever-changing fortunes of history and stands today as one of the most impressive of England's ancient fortresses.

In 1978 Warwick Castle, and the majority of its contents, was acquired by The Tussauds Group, when Lord Brooke, son of the 6th Earl of Warwick, Charles Guy Greville, put it up for sale. Since then over £27 million has been spent on extensive restoration work and much painstaking reconstruction, enabling substantial areas of the Castle to be opened up which were previously closed to the public.

Visitors can enjoy a wide range of attractions within the Castle buildings, which are designed to reflect the various different eras of the Castle's 1,000 year history. The most recent project has been the restoration of the Mill and Engine House. The 14th century mill was originally used for grinding flour; however, in 1894, the innovative Earl of Warwick harnessed the power of the river to generate electricity and light the Castle as a somewhat unusual birthday present for his wife Daisy (also well-known as a favourite of Edward VII, who was a regular visitor).

The 60 acres of grounds are, for many, as much of an attraction as the building itself, which receives over 750,000 visitors every year. There is the informal Pageant Field in a 'Capability' Brown landscape; the Peacock Garden, and the beautiful Victorian rose garden, restored in 1986 and reopened by Diana, Princess of Wales. For those with plenty of energy, a climb up the Castle's imposing towers and a stroll along the battlements provides the perfect view of the grounds and the surrounding countryside.

Sarah Montgomery

Sarah Montgomery
General Manager – Warwick Castle

Weston Park

Shifnal, Shropshire

Royalty, politics, drama and tragedy all feature throughout Weston Park's long and rich history, the house being first mentioned in the Domesday Book in the 11th century. Weston is unusual as one of the few country houses to have been designed by a woman and owes much of its unique charm to the vision of the remarkable Lady Wilbraham, wife of the 2nd Earl of Bradford (1st creation). She was a keen student of architecture, particularly Palladio's *First Book of Architecture*, and in 1671 began directing the building of the present house on the site of an earlier medieval manor.

For centuries, politicians have stayed at Weston Park and Disraeli was a frequent visitor who appreciated the splendours of the house. *"You will find Weston beautiful. I marvel whether I shall ever see the like of it again! It is a place that always pleased me"*.

The 3rd Countess, Selina's, platonic friendship with the widowed Disraeli resulted in a great deal of correspondence – over 1,000 letters – reporting on the gossip of politics, his comings and goings and the reaction of Queen Victoria to events of the day. Another gift from the Prime Minister to the 3rd Countess was a curious one – a yellow parrot. The parrot was thought to be a male until, remarkably, it laid 23 eggs in 24 days. As a result of this enormous effort the parrot died, and the amazing bird and its eggs may be seen displayed in a glass case.

In the 18th century, Lancelot 'Capability' Brown was commissioned by Sir Henry Bridgeman to create the landscaped gardens surrounding the house. Ha-has were constructed, the Temple Pool created and walks and breathtaking vistas gradually emerged as the gardens matured.

During the summer, the House and Park are open to the public to enjoy the beautiful interiors and collections as well as the sweeping landscape, formal gardens, lakes, follies and nature walks. Primarily the House is used on an exclusive residential basis for company meetings, weddings and special events. Weston Park is the result of centuries of creativity, collecting and patronage of artists and craftsmen, by generations of one family, the Bridgemans, Earls of Bradford. Gifted to the nation by Richard, the 7th and present Earl of Bradford, it is now in the care of the Trustees of the Weston Park Foundation.

William Montgomery

William Montgomery
Chairman, The Weston Park Foundation

Wilton House

Salisbury, Wiltshire

Wilton House stands on the site of a 12th century abbey which, with its estate of almost 50,000 acres, was given to William Herbert by Henry VIII in 1542 at the time of the Dissolution of the Monasteries. William, who came from an ancient family of Welsh noblemen, was a great favourite of the King and married Anne Parr, sister of Catherine, Henry's sixth wife.

William quickly demolished the abbey and replaced it with a fine Tudor house and walled courtyard. He received a knighthood in 1543 and then, in 1551, he was created Lord Herbert of Cardiff and Earl of Pembroke in the same week! By passing from father to son, or brother to brother, the line has remained unbroken for over 450 years and the house continuously lived in by the Herbert family throughout that time. Only the central section of the Tudor house remains and the estate now comprises about 14,000 acres.

In 1632, the 4th Earl replaced most of the Tudor house, employing as his architect Isaac de Caus, who also designed a large and elaborate formal garden. After a serious fire in 1647 had destroyed much of the uncompleted structure, a new architect, Inigo Jones, was asked to rebuild the house. The existing south front and the State Rooms, including the great Double Cube room, are the result of his work, aided by his nephew, John Webb. Further alterations were made in the early part of the 19th century by James Wyatt, most significantly the addition of the inner cloisters.

Throughout the generations a fine collection of paintings, furniture and sculpture was built up, most of which remains today. Most notable is the huge Van Dyck painting of the 4th Earl and his family, and the superbly crafted Violin Cabinet made by Thomas Chippendale.

The formal garden was replaced in the 1730s by a landscape garden of lawns and cedar trees, the focal point of which is the beautiful Palladian bridge, designed by Henry, the 9th Earl and his architect Roger Morris. In recent years a forecourt garden, water garden and Millennium water feature have been added.

Pembroke

The Earl of Pembroke

Wolterton Park

Erpingham, Norfolk

The Walpole family had been established in Norfolk for 500 years when Horatio, 1st Lord Walpole and diplomat brother of England's first Prime Minster, Sir Robert Walpole, purchased a small estate at Wolterton in the 1720s.

In subsequent centuries, the Walpoles followed the fashions of their times and thus the landscape today has been constantly shaped and reshaped by owners and tenants. The lake in its present form was created in the 1720s from an earlier feature in front of the old Hall referred to as a 'canal'. Although some Charles Bridgeman drawings exist, it appears that much of the original landscape was done by the Hall's multi-talented architect, Thomas Ripley.

When Horatio bought the Estate, it appears that the old Hall was in a poor state and he commissioned Thomas Ripley to undertake repairs. Ripley suffered from his involvement with the Walpole family in that when they fell from political power, so he fell from grace, but more recently his innovative ideas have been acknowledged. In 1724, there was a fire in the Hall. Subsequently Ripley wrote to Horatio: *"I am sorry for your loss, but since this has happened…I believe you will find a more convenient place for your house…"*. It seems that Horatio agreed, for the present Hall, a Palladian villa, is on a different site to the north west.

Less than 100 years later, Wolterton was abandoned when the 4th Earl of Orford (1813 – 1894) made nearby Mannington his country seat. The house was left empty and many of the contents sold. In the early 20th century his nephew, the 5th Earl, restored the house and, his young son having died, left the property in 1928 to his nearest male relative, my father. During the Second World War the house was occupied, firstly by evacuees and later by the army. However in 1950 it was one of the earliest 'stately homes' to open to the public.

By the time I inherited the house, a major overhaul was once again needed. The first task was to try to find out more about the house's history and this process is still continuing.

The design of the garden has varied with changing fashion but is now returned to 18th century simplicity. The four acre kitchen garden has been in continuous use since the Hall's construction – it is now run as an organic garden, supplying local people through a box scheme.

Address Book

Much of the information shown here has been extracted from *Hudson's Historic Houses & Gardens*, the annual guide which contains full details of properties open to the public in Britain (www.hudsons.co.uk).

Alnwick Castle

Alnwick
Northumberland
NE66 1NQ

tel   01665 510777
info   01665 511100
fax   01665 510876

enquiries@alnwickcastle.com
www.alnwickcastle.com
www.alnwickgarden.com
OS Ref NU187 135

Belmont

Faversham
Kent
ME13 0HH

tel   01795 890202
fax   01795 890042

belmontadmin@btconnect.com
www.belmont-house.org
OS Ref TQ986 564

Borde Hill Gardens

Haywards Heath
West Sussex
RH16 1XP

tel   01444 450326
fax   01444 440427

info@bordehill.co.uk
www.bordehill.co.uk
OS Ref TQ324 265

Burton Agnes Hall

Driffield
East Yorkshire
YO25 0ND

tel   01262 490324
fax   01262 490513

burton.agnes@farmline.com
www.burton-agnes.com
OS Ref TA103 633

Arbury Hall

Nuneaton
Warwickshire
CV10 7PT

tel   024 7638 2804
fax   024 7664 1147

brenda.newell@arburyhall.net
OS Ref SP335 893

Blair Castle

Pitlochry
Perthshire
PH18 5TL

tel   01796 481207
fax   01796 481487

manager@blair-castle.co.uk
www.blair-castle.co.uk
OS Ref NN880 660

Bowood House

Calne
Wiltshire
SN11 0LZ

tel   01249 812102
fax   01249 821757

houseandgardens@bowood.org
www.bowood.org
OS Ref ST974 700

Castle Howard

York
North Yorkshire
YO60 7DA

tel   01653 648333
fax   01653 648501

house@castlehoward.co.uk
www.castlehoward.co.uk
OS Ref SE716 701

Athelhampton House & Gardens

Dorchester
Dorset
DT2 7LG

tel   01305 848363
fax   01305 848135

enquiries@athelhampton.co.uk
www.athelhampton.co.uk
OS Ref SY771 942

Blairquhan Castle

Maybole
Ayrshire
KA19 7LZ

tel   01655 770239
fax   01655 770278

enquiries@blairquhan.co.uk
www.blairquhan.co.uk
OS Ref NS 366 055

Breamore House

Fordingbridge
Hampshire
SP6 2DF

tel   01725 512233
fax   01725 512858

breamore@ukonline.co.uk
OS Ref SU152 191

Cawdor Castle

Nairn
Inverness-shire
IV12 5RD

tel   01667 404615
fax   01667 404674

info@cawdorcastle.com
www.cawdorcastle.com
OS Ref NH850 500

Beaulieu

Brockenhurst
Hampshire
SO42 7ZN

tel   01590 614604
fax   01590 612624

conference@beaulieu.co.uk
www.beaulieu.co.uk
OS Ref SU387 025

Blenheim Palace

Woodstock
Oxfordshire
OX20 1PX

tel   01993 811091
fax   01993 813527

admin@ blenheimpalace.com
www.blenheimpalace.com
OS Ref SP441 161

Broughton Castle

Banbury
Oxfordshire
OX15 5EB

tel/fax   01295 276070
             01295 722547

admin@broughtoncastle.demon.co.uk
www.broughtoncastle.demon.co.uk
OS Ref SP418 382

Chavenage

Tetbury
Gloucestershire
GL8 8XP

tel   01666 502329
fax   01453 836778

info@chavenage.com
www.chavenage.com
OS Ref ST872 952

Chiddingstone Castle

Edenbridge
Kent
TN8 7AD
tel 01892 870347
www.chiddingstone-castle.org.uk
OS Ref TQ497 452

Cholmondeley Castle Gardens

Malpas
Cheshire
SY14 8AH
tel 01829 720383
fax 01829 720877
OS Ref SJ540 515

Cothay Manor

Wellington
Somerset
TA21 0JR
tel 01823 672283
fax 01823 672345
OS Ref ST721 214

Cottesbrooke Hall & Gardens

Cottesbrooke
Northamptonshire
NN6 8PF
tel 01604 505808
fax 01604 505619
hall@cottesbrooke.co.uk
www.cottesbrookehall.co.uk
OS Ref SP711 739

Coughton Court

Alcester
Warwickshire
B49 5JA
tel 01789 400777
fax 01789 765544
info 01789 762435
sales@throckmortons.co.uk
www.coughtoncourt.co.uk
OS Ref SP080 604

Deene Park

Corby
Northamptonshire
NN17 3EW
tel 01780 450278
01780 450223
fax 01780 450282
admin@deenepark.com
www.deenepark.com
OS Ref SP950 929

Dorney Court

Windsor
Berkshire
SL4 6QP
tel 01628 604638
fax 01628 665772
palmer@dorneycourt.co.uk
www.dorneycourt.co.uk
OS Ref SU926 791

Duart Castle

Isle of Mull
Argyll
PA64 6AP
tel 01680 812309
01577 830311
duartguide@isle-of-mull.demon.co.uk
www.duartcastle.com
OS Ref NM750 350

Duncombe Park

Helmsley
North Yorkshire
YO62 5EB
tel 01439 770213
fax 01439 771114
sally@duncombepark.com
www.duncombepark.com
OS Ref SE604 830

Dunrobin Castle

Golspie
Sutherland
KW10 6SF
tel 01408 633177
fax 01408 634081
keith@dunrobin442.fs.life.co.uk
www.highlandescape.com
OS Ref NC850 010

Dunvegan Castle

Isle of Skye
IV55 8WF
tel 01470 521206
fax 01470 521205
info@dunvegancastle.com
www.dunvegancastle.com
OS Ref NG250 480

Eastnor Castle

Ledbury
Herefordshire
HR8 1RL
tel 01531 633160
fax 01531 631776
enquiries@eastnorcastle.com
www.eastnorcastle.com
OS Ref SO735 368

Eyam Hall

Hope Valley
Derbyshire
S32 5QW
tel 01433 631976
fax 01433 631603
nicola@eyamhall.com
www.eyamhall.com
OS Ref OS119 SK216 765

Fasque

Laurencekirk
Kincardineshire
AB30 1DN
tel/fax 01561 340569
tel 01561 340202
OS Ref NO648 755

Floors Castle

Kelso
Roxburghshire
TD5 7SF
tel 01573 223333
fax 01573 226056
jpotts@floorscastle.com
www.floorscastle.com
OS Ref NT711 347

Fonmon Castle

Barry
South Glamorgan
CF62 3ZN
tel 01446 710206
fax 01446 711687
sophie@fonmoncastle.fsnet.co.uk
OS Ref ST047 681

Address Book

Glamis Castle

Forfar
Angus
DD8 1RJ
tel 01307 840393
fax 01307 840733
admin@glamis-castle.co.uk
www.glamis-castle.co.uk
OS Ref NO386 480

Hergest Croft Gardens

Kington
Herefordshire
HR5 3EG
tel 01544 230160
fax 01544 232031
gardens@hergest.kc3.co.uk
www.hergest.co.uk
OS Ref SO281 565

Holker Hall

Grange-over-Sands
Cumbria
LA11 7PL
tel 01539 558328
fax 01539 558378
publicopening@holker.co.uk
www.holker-hall.co.uk
OS Ref SD359 773

Hutton-in-the-Forest

Penrith
Cumbria
CA11 9TH
tel 01768 484449
fax 01768 484571
hutton-in-the-forest@talk21.com
www.hutton-in-the-forest.co.uk
OS Ref NY460 358

Glynde Place

Lewes
East Sussex
BN8 6SX
tel 01273 858224
fax 01273 858224
hampden@glyndeplace.co.uk
OS Ref TQ457 093

Hever Castle

Edenbridge
Kent
TN8 7NG
infoline 01732 865224
fax 01732 866796
mail@hevercastle.co.uk
www.hevercastle.co.uk
OS Ref TQ476 450

Holkham Hall

Wells-next-the-Sea
Norfolk
NR23 1AB
tel 01328 710227
fax 01328 711707
p.minchin@holkham.co.uk
www.holkham.co.uk
OS Ref TF885 428

Inveraray Castle

Inveraray
Argyll
PA32 8XE
tel 01499 302203
fax 01499 302421
enquiries@inveraray-castle.com
www.inveraray-castle.com
OS Ref. NN100 090

Haddon Hall

Bakewell
Derbyshire
DE45 1LA
tel 01629 812855
fax 01629 814379
info@haddonhall.co.uk
www.haddonhall.co.uk
OS Ref SK234 663

Highclere Castle

Newbury
Berkshire
RG20 9RN
tel 01635 253210
fax 01635 255315
theoffice@highclerecastle.co.uk
www.highclerecastle.co.uk
OS Ref SU445 587

Hopetoun House

South Queensferry
West Lothian
EH30 9SL
tel 0131 331 2451
fax 0131 319 1885
marketing@hopetounhouse.com
www.hopetounhouse.com
OS Ref NT089 790

Kentwell Hall

Long Melford
Suffolk
CO10 9BA
tel 01787 310207
fax 01787 379318
info@kentwell.co.uk
www.kentwell.co.uk
OS Ref TL864 479

Hamptworth Lodge

Salisbury
Wiltshire
SP5 2EA
tel 01794 390215
fax 01794 390700
OS Ref SU227 195

Hoghton Tower

Preston
Lancashire
PR5 0SH
tel 01254 852986
fax 01254 852109
OS Ref SD622 264

Houghton Hall

King's Lynn
Norfolk
PE31 6UE
tel 01485 528569
fax 01485 528167
enquiries@houghtonhall.com
www.houghtonhall.com
OS Ref TF792 287

Layer Marney Tower

Colchester
Essex
CO5 9US
tel/fax 01206 330784
info@layermarneytower.co.uk
www.layermarneytower.co.uk
OS Ref TL929 175

Leeds Castle

Maidstone
Kent
ME17 1PL
tel   01622 765400
fax   01622 735616
enquiries@leeds-castle.com
www.leeds-castle.com
OS Ref TQ835 533

Lulworth Castle

Wareham
Dorset
BH20 5QS
tel   01929 400352
fax   01929 400563
estate.office@lulworth.com
www.lulworth.com
OS194 Ref SY853 822

Muncaster Castle

Ravenglass
Cumbria
CA18 1RQ
tel   01229 717614
fax   01229 717010
info@muncaster.co.uk
www.muncaster.co.uk
OS Ref SD103 965

Pencarrow

Bodmin
Cornwall
PL30 3AG
tel   01208 841369
fax   01208 841722
pencarrow@aol.com
www.pencarrow.co.uk
OS Ref SX040 711

Leighton Hall

Carnforth
Lancashire
LA5 9ST
tel   01524 734474
fax   01524 720357
info@leightonhall.co.uk
www.leightonhall.co.uk
OS Ref SD494 744

Manderston

Duns
Berwickshire
TD11 3PP
tel   01361 883450
secretary 01361 882636
fax   01361 882010
palmer@manderston.co.uk
www.manderston.co.uk
OS Ref NT810 544

Newby Hall

Ripon
North Yorkshire
HG4 5AE
tel   01423 322583
fax   01423 324452
info@newbyhall.com
www.newbyhall.com
OS Ref. SE348 675

Powderham Castle

Exeter
Devon
EX6 8JQ
tel   01626 890243
fax   01626 890729
castle@powderham.co.uk
www.powderham.co.uk
OS Ref SX965 832

Levens Hall

Kendal
Cumbria
LA8 0PD
tel   01539 560321
fax   01539 560669
email@levenshall.fsnet.co.uk
www.levenshall.co.uk
OS Ref SD495 851

Mannington Hall

Saxthorpe
Norfolk   NR11 7BB
tel   01263 584175
fax   01263 761214
OS Ref TG144 320

Norton Conyers

Ripon
North Yorkshire
HG4 5EQ
tel/fax 01765 640333
norton.conyers@ripon.org
OS Ref SF319 763

Prideaux Place

Padstow
Cornwall
PL28 8RP
tel   01841 532411
fax   01841 532945
office@prideauxplace.fsnet.co.uk
OS Ref SW913 756

Longleat

Warminster
Wiltshire
BA12 7NW
tel   01985 844400
fax   01985 844885
enquiries@longleat.co.uk
www.longleat.co.uk
OS Ref ST809 430

Mellerstain

Gordon
Berwickshire
TD3 6LG
tel   01573 410225
fax   01573 410636
enquiries@mellerstain.com
www.mellerstain.com
OS Ref NT648 392.

Pashley Manor Gardens

Ticehurst
East Sussex
TN5 7HE
tel   01580 200888
fax   01580 200102
info@pashleymanorgardens.com
www.pashleymanorgardens.com
OS Ref TQ 707 291

Raby Castle

Darlington
Co Durham
DL2 3AH
tel   01833 660202
fax   01833 660169
admin@rabycastle.com
www.rabycastle.com
OS Ref NZ129 218

Address Book

Rockingham Castle
Market Harborough
Leicestershire
LE16 8TH
tel 01536 770240
fax 01536 771692
estateoffice@rockinghamcastle.com
www.rockinghamcastle.com
OS Ref SP867 913

Somerleyton Hall
Lowestoft
Suffolk
NR32 5QQ
tel 01502 730224
fax 01502 732143
enquiries@somerleyton.co.uk
www.somerleyton.co.uk
OS134 Ref TM493 977

Stobhall
Guildtown
Perthshire
PH2 6DR
tel 01821 640332
OS Ref NO132 343

Thorp Perrow Arboretum
Bedale
North Yorkshire
DL8 2PR
tel/fax 01677 425323
louise@thorpperrow.com
www.thorpperrow.com
OS Ref SE258 851

Rode Hall
Scholar Green
Cheshire
ST7 3QP
tel 01270 873237
fax 01270 882962
rodehall@scholargreen.fsnet.co.uk
OS Ref SJ819 573

Squerryes Court
Westerham
Kent
TN16 1SJ
tel 01959 562345
01959 563118
fax 01959 565949
squerryes.court@squerryes.co.uk
www.squerryes.co.uk
OS Ref TQ440 535

Stonor Park
Henley-on-Thames
Oxfordshire
tel 01491 638587
fax 01491 639348
jweaver@stonor.com
www.stonor.com
OS Ref SU743 893

Tissington Hall
Ashbourne
Derbyshire
DE6 1RA
tel 01335 352200
fax 01335 352201
tisshall@dircon.co.uk
www.tissington-hall.com
OS Ref SK175 524

Sand
Sidmouth
Devon
EX10 0QN
tel 01395 597230
sand@eastdevon.net
www.eastdevon.net/sand
OS Ref SY146 925

Stanford Hall
Lutterworth
Leicestershire
LE17 6DH
tel 01788 860250
fax 01788 860870
enquiries@stanfordhall.co.uk
www.stanfordhall.co.uk
OS Ref SP587 793

Stratfield Saye
Basingstoke
Hampshire
RG7 2BZ
tel 01256 882882
www.stratfield-saye.co.uk
OS Ref SU700 615

Torosay Castle
Isle of Mull
Argyll
PA65 6AY
tel 01680 812421
fax 01680 812470
torosay@aol.com
www.holidaymull.org/members/torosay
OS Ref NM730 350

Scone Palace
Perth
Perthshire
PH2 6BD
tel 0845 1261060
fax 01738 552588
visits@scone-palace.co.uk
www.scone-palace.co.uk
OS Ref NO114 266

Stanway House & Water Garden
Cheltenham
Gloucestershire
GL54 5PQ
tel 01386 584469
fax 01386 584688
stanwayhouse@btinternet.com
OS Ref SP061 323

Syon House
Brentford
Middlesex
TW8 8JF
tel 020 8560 0882
fax 020 8568 0936
info@syonpark.co.uk
www.syonpark.co.uk
OS Ref TQ173 767

Traquair
Innerleithen
Peeblesshire
EH44 6PW
tel 01896 830323
fax 01896 830639
enquiries@traquair.co.uk
www.traquair.co.uk
OS Ref NY330 354

Warwick Castle

Warwick
CV34 4QU
tel   0870 442 2000
fax   01926 401692
customer.information@warwick-castle.com
www.warwick-castle.co.uk
OS Ref SP284 648

Weston Park

Weston-under-Lizard
Shifnal
Shropshire
TF11 8LE
tel   01952 852100
fax   01952 850430
enquiries@weston-park.com
www.weston-park.com
OS Ref SJ808 107

Wilton House

Salisbury
Wiltshire
SP2 0BJ
tel   01722 746720
fax   01722 744447
tourism@wiltonhouse.com
www.wiltonhouse.com
OS Ref SU099 311

Wolterton Park

Erpingham
Norfolk
NR11 7BB
tel   01263 584175
fax   01263 761214
OS Ref TG164 317

Photographic Credits

Aerial Images

This book was initiated and the aerial photography managed by Andy and Brenda Marks of Skyscan, who would like to thank colleagues for their skill in producing these wonderful photographs despite the uncertainties of the weather. All the images were taken from light aircraft, except those created with the Skyscan™ balloon camera unit, as credited below.

pp 17, 23, 31, 47, 53, 57, 59, 81, 89, 91, 101, 107, 109, 111, 123, 133, 143, 151, 153, 155, 163, 175 & 181
Nigel Stockwell and photographer Kevin Allen of London Aerial Photo Library

pp 39, 49, 63, 71, 83, 93, 115, 129, 131, 145 & 169
Will Cross of Skycam UK

pp 19, 21, 33, 35, 45, 51, 69, 77, 85, 87, 117, 119, 135, 137, 139, 147, 177 & 179
Bob Evans of Bristol & West Photography

pp 27, 43, 61, 65, 73, 95, 99, 103, 105, 113, 125, 127, 141, 159, 167, 171 & 173
Bill Henderson of Air Images

p 67 – Robbie West of West Photo

p 15 – Andy Marks of Skyscan (in collaboration with Ron Bridle of Sky Eye Aerial Photography)

pp 25, 29, 37, 41, 55, 75, 79, 97, 121, 157, 161, 165 & back cover – Andy Marks of Skyscan

All the aerial images which appear in this book are the copyright of Skyscan who hold them in their specialist aerial and aviation photolibrary. Their web site at *www.skyscan.co.uk* shows many of the images from this, previous books and other publications.

Other Images